Media Studies for GCSE
Teaching Pack

PETER WALL
CHIEF EXAMINER

Published by Collins Educational
An imprint of HarperCollins*Publishers* Ltd
77–85 Fulham Palace Road
London W6 8JB

© Peter Wall 1999, 2002 (new edition)

First published 1999
ISBN 000 713392 8

10 9 8 7 6 5 4 3

Peter Wall asserts the moral right to be identified as the author of this work.

British Library Cataloguing in Publication Data
A catalogue record for this book is available from the British Library.

Commissioning Editor: Helen Clark
Project Management: Charlie Evans
Edited by Charlie Evans and Charlie Rundall
Cover design: Caroline Grimshaw
Internal design: Jenny Fleet
Cover photo: Getty images
Illustrations: Harry Venning, Clinton Banbury and Chris Pavely
Permissions cleared by Gavin Jones
Production: Katie Morris
Printed and bound by Martins the Printers, Berwick upon Tweed

Contents

Syllabus coverage chart

Together, *Media Studies for GCSE* and this *Media Studies for GCSE Teaching Pack* form a complete course. The chart shows how the two books cover the OCR, WJEC and AQA GCSE Media Studies syllabuses.

Syllabus element	AQA	WJEC	OCR
Language	✓	✓ Media forms and representations	✓ Languages and categories
Representation	✓	✓ Media forms and representations	✓ Media messages and values
Institutions	✓	✓ Media organisations	✓ Media producers and audiences
Audience	✓	✓ Media audiences	✓ Media producers and audiences
Production and evaluation	✓	✓	✓ Practical tasks and evaluative commentary
Case studies (Television news; Cinema; Newspapers, magazines and comics; Music industry; Radio; Advertising)	**All relevant** **2003** Comedy Films (available as a download from www.collinseducation.co.uk) **2004** Local and community radio	**2003** **Section B** Newspapers **2004** **Section A** Television news **Section B** Print-based advertisements **2005** **Section B** Magazines	**2003 and 2004** **Components 1 and 2** (Moving Image Option) **Components 3 and 4** (Print Option) 2003 and 2004 – Teenage Magazines **Components 5 and 6** 2003 and 2004 – News (television, newspapers, radio and the Internet) Advertising (television, cinema, print, radio, and the Internet)
Assignments	✓	✓ Coursework	✓ Practical/coursework
Controlled test	✓	n/a	n/a

Teacher's notes

The following icons are used:

 On your own

 As a class

 In pairs

 Homework

 In groups

 Relevant section of textbook

1. Why Media Studies?

Media Studies is a potentially vast area, especially where syllabuses are open-ended and provide opportunities for exploration across a range of media forms. It is important that students have some sense of the territory covered by the discipline. It is also important to establish early in the course the significance of Media Studies as part of the curriculum. This can be achieved to some degree by focusing on the role that it plays in the lives not only of the students themselves, but of the population as a whole.

Worksheets 1–3, therefore, provide students with an opportunity to define the area that Media Studies is likely to explore, and to consider the significance of media products in their own lives and those of other people. The worksheets, which students could do even before they read the chapter, lend themselves to further work, analysing and presenting the information obtained through their research. This might take the form of charts for display on the classroom walls.

You and the media

Worksheet 1 should form a useful introduction to the areas to be covered during the course. It may also help the teacher identify aspects of the media that are of particular interest both for individuals and for the class as a whole; this can be useful in determining the kind of work that may be introduced later in the course. The worksheet also provides an opportunity to raise at an early stage some of the central issues of the course, by considering how media texts impact upon the lives of those who consume them. In addition, it allows teachers to reinforce the centrality of media to contemporary life.

How different people view the media

Worksheet 2 broadens the area of consideration by asking students to think about how people of different ages, genders and backgrounds relate to media products, and how these products affect their lives. This will signal an important shift away from a peer group focus to the notion of a wider, potentially segmented audience for media products. Introducing the questionnaire should underline the significance of collecting information about audiences and their preferences, which becomes particularly important in production-based work later in the course.

Diary of media consumption

Worksheet 3, which provides a template for Activities 1 and 2 on page 7 of the textbook, allows students to identify and analyse their own patterns of media consumption. At least one of the three days could usefully be a weekend day, as weekend consumption of the media may be significantly different from weekday consumption. Students could be asked whether they are surprised at the amount and pattern of consumption that their diary reveals, and whether they think they are typical of people their age in these respects. Follow-up work might include class discussion of the factors that determine how and why people consume the media. Later in the course, this can also lead on to work around gratification theory (see pages 66–7 of the textbook) through an exploration of the uses to which media consumption is put.

2. Language

Most students inevitably identify using the media as a recreational activity. Media Studies requires them to see it as an academic activity. The worksheets for chapter 2 aim to provide students with the analytical skills they need to deconstruct media texts. This is an important skill, not least because the media, especially television and film, offer what appears to be a very realistic view of the world. It is essential, therefore, for students to begin to grasp that most media texts have been carefully constructed in order to produce a message for the audience.

Worksheets 4–14 provide students with a basic critical vocabulary which will help them to describe and analyse media messages. The sooner students become familiar with this vocabulary, the sooner they will become confident in dealing with a variety of texts. By looking across a range of media forms and texts, students are also offered the opportunity to identify similarities and differences in how different media forms communicate with an audience.

Image analysis   4

A reliable place to start textual analysis is by looking at still images. The analysis of the L'Aimant advertisement (textbook pages 14–15) will provide a way into this worksheet. Work on visual language, denotation and connotation and texts (pages 8–13) is also relevant. Ideally the image provided for use with this worksheet should be in colour. As teachers will probably want to use the same image with all of the class, copying the image on to a transparency may be a practical solution, if a full class set is not available.

Anchorage   5

This worksheet provides reinforcement for the 'Caption competition' activity on page 11 of the textbook. For this worksheet, a news photograph can be used with the caption removed. Either the same image or a different image can be used for the cropping exercise, but care should be taken to find an image with a clear indication of a context and/or a number of characters. This will allow students more opportunity to play with the image and its meanings. Students will probably find it useful to work through the paragraph on anchorage on page 11 of the textbook in preparation for this worksheet.

Codes   6

Textual analysis is developed in Worksheet 6, which reinforces the concept of codes. The first task is intended to get students thinking about how a code requires encoding by the sender and decoding by the receiver, and how you need to 'read' a code. The weather chart on page 17 of the textbook is used as the basis for the second task on the sheet. Teachers will also need to provide a pre-recorded extract from an appropriate television programme. Alternatively, teachers with access to foreign language programming may like to use a news bulletin or game show from that source.

Reading the media   7

Worksheet 7 gives students a chance to choose their own images for analysis. Whilst guidance is obviously needed here, it is important for their critical autonomy that they are allowed to determine the agenda at this point. This worksheet should signal the importance of the active reader in relation to textual analysis. Students will benefit from reading pages 8–13 and 14–21 of the textbook before attempting this worksheet. Key issues such as composition and colour can also be explored through the use of 'stills' from film and television: analysis of the moving image obviously overlaps in many areas with work on still images.

Analysing moving images   8a 8b

Worksheets 8a and 8b require the selection of an appropriate sequence recorded from television. Some searching will be needed to locate a sequence that will include the variety of shots and edits required in the worksheet. It may, therefore, be necessary to use two or more sequences for these worksheets. Pages 18–21 of the textbook are useful reading for students working on these sheets.

Advert storyboard   9

This worksheet allows the student to develop the work begun in Worksheet 8 by designing a storyboard. The suggested TV advertisement can readily be replaced with, or supplemented by, a title sequence or trailer. Pages 209–210 of the textbook describe how a basic storyboard is put together.

Narrative   10

Pages 21–26 of the textbook are required reading for this worksheet. Although it offers the student the opportunity to work on a variety of texts, it may be advisable initially for the teacher to suggest a range of texts from which to select. This will help to ensure that the key elements the student is seeking are apparent within the text.

Narrative and genre   11

Worksheet 11 provides a link between work on narrative and the concept of genre by inviting students to consider how a simple narrative might be treated differently across different genres. (Different genres could, of course, be substituted, for example soap, documentary, radio advertisement and tabloid newspaper story.) This worksheet may be used as a follow up to the 'In groups' activity on page 22 of the textbook. Pages 21–29 of the textbook are relevant to Worksheets 11–14.

Icons; Sitcom analysis; Sitcom characters   12 13 14

Worksheets 12–14 provide more detailed work on narrative and genre. Worksheet 12 focuses on the iconography of films, while the focus on situation comedy in Worksheet 13 allows for a range of possible TV and radio options. Worksheet 14 explores the concept of character typology. Worksheets 13 and 14 could be adapted to cover different genres or sub-genres, for example different types of western, and to investigate the problems of texts that exhibit qualities borrowed from a range of genres.

Features of soap operas **15**

Worksheet 15 serves to identify generic features that define soaps. It is possible to develop from this worksheet tasks that emphasise the importance to producers of maintaining these features in order to secure audiences. For example, students can be asked to consider the ways in which new examples of the genre may seek to change existing formulas. Equally, the importance of audience expectations is an area that can usefully be explored.

3. Representation

Student's Book **30-41**

It is important that the potential breadth of this concept is acknowledged. There is often a tendency to limit work on representation to stereotyping; this, although interesting and enjoyable for students, is only part of a complex picture that includes wider issues such as the notion of realism and the selection and structuring of material represented by the media.

Representing you **16**

Worksheet 16 introduces students to the idea of representation by using photographic images of themselves and examining how negative and positive representations can be created. This worksheet could be used instead of, or to support, the 'On your own' activity on page 34 of the textbook.

Re-presentation **17**

Worksheet 17 can be used alongside, or instead of, the 'Group activities' on page 32 of the textbook. It requires the teacher to set up an event or sequence of events, ideally involving a conflict, for the class to witness and report on. It may be possible to use a sequence recorded from a television drama, such as a soap, or to ask a drama group to come into the classroom to perform a sequence. These forms will have the additional advantage of being able to be shown again after the task is completed. The worksheet should demonstrate how an event is reshaped and re-presented in order to fit a particular view of the world. Work on this could be developed to include producing storyboards, scripts and news stories around the same event. In this way, you can show how representation is a crucial issue in all areas of the media.

Techniques of presentation **18**

Worksheet 18 relates closely to some of the work students will have undertaken in the section on media language (chapter 2). A careful choice of text for consideration is important here. Ideally the techniques of sound, camerawork and editing used will be reasonably accessible to the class; you may like to refer students back to the 'Image analysis' section of the textbook (pages 18–21). This worksheet can also be used as the basis for exploring notions of bias and objectivity in 'factual' programmes. For example, you could ask students to consider how representation affects our understanding of, and attitude to, the issues presented.

Content analysis **19**

Asking students to work in groups for this activity will allow a greater amount of material to be analysed, which should produce a more accurate result. A full week's editions of one or more tabloids can readily be covered by the class. Group work will also provide the opportunity for discussion of how such categories as appearance and age should be classified and described. The worksheet can be modified to work with most visual media, for example television commercials, magazine advertisements or film or video trailers. The worksheet can also be adapted to cover the representation of any group within society. Results of the survey can be presented in the form of wall charts or OHTs as the basis for wide-ranging work on the nature of representation within specific media. Pages 36–7 of the textbook have some helpful suggestions for students carrying out this type of analysis.

Stereotypes;
Are you a stereotype? **20 21**

Worksheet 20 needs to be handled with care, as there is an obvious danger of giving free reign to prejudices that students may be harbouring. It might be useful to direct students to look at specific social groups, rather than allowing them to choose their own. One danger of work on stereotypes is that students fall into the trap of using stereotypes themselves. Worksheet 21 highlights the fact that real people lie beneath stereotypical images by confronting students themselves with their own potential for being stereotyped. Both worksheets should be used alongside the section on stereotypes in the textbook (pages 37–41).

Positive and
negative representations **22**

Worksheet 22 encourages work around positive representations. It also introduces the idea that creating positive representations is often more difficult than using established negative stereotypes. Teachers may wish to replace the storyboard in questions B and C with a magazine cover or film poster design. This worksheet supplements the 'Role-play' activity on page 39 of the textbook.

4. Institutions

42-57

Teaching about institutions in way that interests and engages students presents a challenge for the Media Studies teacher. The temptation to fall back on some knowledge-based approach, such as a history of the BBC, is definitely to be avoided. Instead, a strategy that seeks to bring to life the people, functions and values that make up a media institution will engage students in this sometimes problematic area. Visiting speakers, for example from local radio or the press, can help in this respect. Ideally the area of institutions is best linked to other key concepts, such as audience, rather than being seen as a stand-alone unit.

Institutions 23

Worksheet 23 indicates the relationship between media texts and the institutions that produce them. Students may need some prompting to seek out the information required. Names of production companies, for example, can be found by looking at title credits. The question at the end should draw attention to the difficulty that sometimes exists in tying well-known media products to the institutions that produce them. Teachers may wish their students to consider the significance of cross-media ownership by large media organisations. Worksheet 23 could also reinforce the 'Niches' activity on page 50 of the textbook.

Ownership 24

This worksheet supports pages 42–43 of the textbook. Information about share prices is readily found in the city pages of most broadsheet newspapers. Alternatively, you could use the newspaper clipping shown on page 42 of the textbook. Materials from such organisations as the Campaign for Press and Broadcasting Freedom can be useful in keeping up to date with issues relating to ownership (see Contacts and resources, page 128).

Alternative media 25

This worksheet, which extends the discussion point on page 45 of the textbook, should help to hone students' perceptions of how their own production skills may find a more realistic role within the media. Students could be asked to design a cover and/or an article for the first issue of their fanzine. Suggestions on how to design articles in magazines can be found on pages 217–219 of the textbook. Teachers interested in developing further work on alternative media may like to get in touch with a local community video workshop or similar organisation. A class activity in the form of a screening of some material, or even a visit from one of the organisers, can be a stimulating learning experience.

Job adverts 26

Worksheet 26 considers the type of people who are likely to get jobs in media institutions. It invites students to consider if certain types of people are more often employed than others. The Media Guardian (Mondays) or any of the media sections from the other broadsheets are a useful source of media jobs to be used as the basis for work on this sheet. Alternatively, the job adverts on pages 46 of the textbook could be used. Worksheet 26 supplements the 'On your own' activity on page 46 of the textbook.

Applying for a job; The interview 27

This worksheet gives students a chance to consider how media jobs are filled by means of role-plays in which the qualities considered appropriate can be explored. Teachers may like to use the worksheets as the basis for further class discussion about how candidates are chosen, and whether the qualities sought by students are likely to be the same as those sought by the industry.

Newsreaders and reporters 28

Worksheet 28 looks at the idea of a code of professional practice. An exploration of the presentational codes behind the news on the three TV channels should raise for students the issue of how far these codes determine the content and nature of media messages such as news bulletins. Students could list the similarities and differences between the news bulletins and discuss why newsreaders shared certain qualities. Relevant reading can be found on pages 45–47 of the textbook.

Costing a video film 29

Worksheet 29 uses video production as an example of costing a media enterprise. Rate cards detailing hire costs of equipment should be readily available from local facilities houses (usually listed under Video Services in the Yellow Pages or in trade magazines). It may be helpful to suggest to students rates of pay for technical staff. The worksheet has the added benefit of making students aware of just how expensive media production costs are. It is to be hoped that they may bear this in mind when negotiating for the use of equipment for their own production work! Pages 44–49 of the textbook are relevant background reading for this worksheet.

Popularity and success 30

Students have the opportunity to undertake research in this worksheet; most of the information should be readily available from such sources as the Radio Times, or the media supplements in the broadsheets (especially the Media Guardian, published on Mondays) or the trade press. The Audit Bureau of Circulation (www.abc.org.uk/) has a searchable database of circulation statistics for print publications. Popularity and success are discussed on pages 47–51 of the textbook; this worksheet could also be used to reinforce the information and activities on pages 66–9.

Scheduling 31

Worksheet 31, which provides follow-on work for the activities on pages 53–55 of the textbook, focuses on the battle for Saturday night prime-time audiences. The work could be extended by looking at actual examples of the programmes, and inviting class discussion about their appeal to the family audience. For example, students may like to consider the emphasis on shows that feature families, and to identify which elements of programmes have an appeal to specific members of the family.

Controlling institutions 32

Discussing the regulation of the media provides many opportunities to link work with the concept of audience, particularly in terms of censorship issues. Most of the regulatory bodies produce useful materials and reports, and many have teacher- and student-friendly websites (see Contacts and resources, pages 125–126). Relevant reading for this worksheet are pages 55–7 of the textbook. Information about controlling institutions is also given on pages 58–63 of the textbook. The names of the institutions required for Question A are, in order: Ofcom, BBFC, PCC, Ofcom, BBFC, Ofcom, ASA, Ofcom.

5. Audience

Audience provides Media Studies with one of its key defining characteristics, yet it is also an area easily overlooked by teachers in their focus on textual analysis. It is important to identify for students the diversity of audiences that consume the media. Students too readily perceive the audience as comprising merely themselves and their peers. While it can be fruitful to encourage them to think in terms of the needs of this audience, attention should also be focused on how the needs of other and different audiences are met by media output.

Media profile 33

The aim of this worksheet is get students to consider how different people use and consume media products. Work around lifestyle would make a useful introduction to the worksheet. For example, a person's job, income, domestic situation, aspirations and background may be considered, as well as their leisure interests. The worksheet can also then be used to develop an exploration of the relationship between lifestyle and individual media consumption.

The watershed and violence 34

This worksheet, which extends the activity on page 59 of the textbook, tackles a central theme in audience work – the effects debate. The watershed is an important concept in the control of the material available to television audiences. Copies of listings magazines are useful for looking at programmes shown before and after the watershed.

Age-appropriate 35

Worksheet 35, which relates to pages 58–60 of the textbook, offers a direct and lively way of pursuing the issue of censorship, using materials close to the cultural experiences of the students themselves. Censorship is a sensitive area, which many teachers may wish to avoid, especially where students are being invited to introduce material into the classroom themselves. Teachers may therefore prefer to select and prepare the material themselves for use with this worksheet.

Audience participation 36

Audience participation offers a rich source of teaching materials across a range of media forms. Teachers may like to focus upon a specific genre, such as the docu-soap, to explore this area in greater depth. This worksheet reinforces the 'Group discussion' activity on page 65 of the textbook.

Audience segmentation 37

Segmentation can be approached from either the focus of institutions or, as here, through audience. Either way, it provides opportunities for looking at the decline of mass audiences in favour of the targeting of more specific interest groups. Copies of satellite channel listings and examples of specialist magazines are useful stimulus material for this worksheet, which supports pages 64–65 of the textbook.

Having your say 38

This worksheet, which supports pages 65–67 of the textbook, focuses attention on the power of the audience to affect media output. It may be useful to show students examples of some of the feedback that the media receives, for example through the letters column of a newspaper, or through a recording of a programme such as *Right to Reply*. The worksheet could be extended to consider the increasing role of the public in the media output, by linking it to Worksheet 36 which looks at audience participation. Equally it could serve as a starting-point for work on the regulation and control of media organisations, through linking it to Worksheet 32.

Audience positioning   **39**

Worksheet 39 requires a recording of a wildlife programme. Students are asked to explore how audiences are positioned to respond to conflict within the narratives offered. The worksheet could be adapted to cover other types of programme, such as documentaries. Audience positioning is discussed on pages 69–71 of the textbook; this worksheet can also be used alongside the 'On your own' activity on page 25 of the textbook.

Conditions of consumption   **40**

Worksheet 40, which relates to pages 71–3 of the textbook, raises the important debate around media consumption within the context of the family (or whatever social group the student is located in). It offers opportunities to develop work around how the context in which media is consumed can affect its meaning. For example, students may find that a programme viewed with friends or in the classroom may deliver a different message when watched as part of a family.

6. Cinema

76-93

It is not uncommon to find that whilst many students know a lot about film, they may have a very limited experience of going to the cinema. This is especially true with the trend of siting many multiplex cinemas out of town, which can make access without a car difficult. It can be a valuable learning experience to give students the opportunity to visit a cinema. It is better still if this can be organised on the basis of a guided tour, together with the screening of a film. It may also be possible to persuade the manager of a local cinema to come in and talk to a class about how films are screened and distributed.

Your local cinemas   **41**

It would be useful to provide photocopies of a map of the local area to an appropriate scale to help with this task. Alternatively, make an OHT of the local area and mark local cinemas on it. Work around the commercial distribution of films and independent cinema could be developed in regions where there is a variety of cinemas to compare. Worksheet 2 is likely to produce a wide variety of responses according to the geographical location of students.

The top five films   **42**

Worksheet 53 could obviously be used as the basis for work relating to a cinema visit. If a visit is not possible, it can equally well be developed using material from the local press, or publicity material from the cinemas themselves. This worksheet could be used to follow on from the 'On your own' activity on page 113 of the textbook. Genre is discussed on pages 27–29 of the textbook.

Viewing conditions   **43**

This worksheet explores the consumption of films other than in the cinema. It is possible to develop work on how changing technologies may influence consumption by considering how closely the viewing of films at home reflects the cinematic experience. Students should be asked to consider some of the points raised on page 83 of the textbook before responding to this worksheet. Pages 72–5 are also relevant to this issue.

My ideas for a movie   **44**

Students usually enjoy the opportunity to develop their own ideas in relation to cinema. Worksheet 44 provides the chance to do just that, whilst at the same time providing a framework that makes the work accessible and keeps the outcome within reasonable limits. Students will need a couple of sheets of storyboard paper (Worksheet 9) to complete the tasks. Teachers may wish to develop a more sustained piece of work around this worksheet, perhaps by exploring the use of stars, or even film finance. It could also be used as a shortened version of a controlled test practice exercise or even mock exam.

Marketing a film   **45**

This worksheet encourages students to think about how audiences choose the films they watch. It provides an opportunity to explore the relationship between what is critical judgement and what is mere promotion. Marketing is covered on pages 88–91 of the textbook; the star system is also discussed on pages 48–49.

7. Media technology

94-107

Media technology   **46**

This worksheet is obviously going to require students to have access to the Internet. Working in pairs or groups of three may relieve some congestion on computers. Many teachers may prefer a fairly structured approach where websites are downloaded on to disk in advance and print versions made available to the students. Teachers confident with the technology may also like to consider giving students the opportunity to pursue the design work, using some of the readily available website design software.

Using new technology   **47**

This is probably best set as a small group activity as students are likely to have different experiences of media technology. They should be encouraged to think across a range of consumer contexts rather than simply considering what is available in the home. The results of the survey might form a classroom display especially if some illustration of the latest technology can be incorporated. This display might then act as stimulus for further work on the impact of media technology on our lives.

Technology on the move 48

Another activity that is probably best handled in groups as some students will have more experience of mobile phone technology than others. Groups can feed back to the whole class and perhaps stimulate some discussion and activities based on targeting audiences and the media's invasion of privacy.

Where will technology lead us? 49

This activity is probably best set for work in pairs or a small group. This will give students a chance to bounce ideas off each other. Students should be encouraged to look at the latest technology available now perhaps by encouraging them to visit local retailers with state of the art equipment. Further work might be based on the issue of the benefits and downside of technological change.

8. Newspapers, magazines and comics

Newspapers

110-139

Work on newspapers can readily be linked to other media forms that provide news. The presentation of news and the nature of news values can be compared across the media of television, radio and newspapers. Work on Teletext and the Internet as sources of news can also be linked in here.

Types of newspapers 50

Worksheet 50 should enable students to explore the range of newspapers available to potential readers. It also considers issues of audience and ownership. The 'typical reader' may be identified by using the scale on page 68 of the textbook. Teachers may wish to take this a stage further by considering political allegiance within the press: the information on pages 42–43 of the textbook provides a useful context for such a discussion. Types of newspaper are described in the textbook on pages 111–113. An example of a freesheet – a title distributed free, usually by a local newspaper group – could be taken into the classroom if students are uncertain about this type of newspaper.

Front page 51a 51b

Worksheet 51a focuses on the construction of the front page of a newspaper. Teachers may wish to use the front page of one newspaper as a means of establishing how the worksheet should be used, before asking their students to choose their own title for analysis. If each

group of students is guided to a different front page, the class discussion could focus in part on the similarities and differences in design and content. The labelled front page of a newspaper on page 124 of the textbook provides a visual guide to the vocabulary used to describe newspaper layouts.

Worksheet 51b can be used as an extension to the 'in pairs' exercise on p123. The original headlines were: 1. Copper load of our Lisa. 2. Till Deaf Do Us Part. 3. Miss PC World.

Analysing a newspaper story 52

The detailed analysis of a specific story follows on naturally from Worksheet 51. Some production-based work relating to students writing their own story, or rewriting an existing story in the style of another title, can also be useful. This can be further developed with layout work using either cut and paste or on-screen page make-up. Newspaper stories are discussed in detail on pages 119–123 of the textbook.

Who does what in newspapers? 53

Newspapers, with their reasonably clearly defined hierarchies and job roles, provide an opportunity for the study of the organisational aspects of media institutions. This worksheet supports pages 113–117 of the textbook.

Magazines

127-132

This is a popular area of study: magazine work is used extensively by students, especially in coursework. Some detailed consideration of magazines as a mass media form can, therefore, be of great value.

Types of magazines 54

Worksheet 54, which supports pages 127–128 of the textbook, gets students to look at the wide range of magazines that are targeted at particular audiences. Market segmentation, with particular reference to magazines, is also discussed on page 50 of the textbook. If students find it difficult to spend time looking in large newsagent's at the range of titles available, the teacher could acquire a range of titles for all or some of the genres indicated on the worksheet. The tasks on this worksheet could form the basis for some initial research for a student's practical production.

Cover and contents 55

Students will need access to at least one copy of a magazine for Worksheet 55, which calls for some detailed analysis of covers and contents pages. Teachers may wish to look at developing this worksheet further to consider an inside feature. This might be especially useful where students are likely to be undertaking magazine work as their practical production.

Comics

133-139

Comics are a relatively neglected area of study, even though quite a range of titles is still available, some of them having survived from previous eras in spite of technological change.

Types of comics 56

Worksheet 56 asks students to identify the titles currently published and to consider why comics have been such a lasting form in the face of competition from other forms of entertainment.

Codes and conventions in comics 57

You will need to supply a comic strip for students to use with this worksheet, which provides an opportunity to look in detail at how comics 'work'. This can form the basis for an interesting and rewarding study of the codes and conventions of visual narrative. Many students feel that lack of drawing skills is a limiting factor in production work. This worksheet may serve to demonstrate that using the written word, possibly with basic sketches, can easily overcome this. The elements of comics are discussed on pages 135–6 of the textbook.

9. Music industry

140-159

Work on the music industry is most likely to lead to an exploration of popular forms of music. However, this need not necessarily be the case. Although the worksheets readily lend themselves to the study of popular chart music, it should be possible through minor modification to target other types of music, for example, film soundtracks or even classical music. Indeed, the relationship between music and media forms such as cinema and advertising provides rich opportunities for investigation by students.

The music in your life 58

Worksheet 58 aims to help students recognise the diversity of music and musical forms in everyday life. It also encourages them to consider how much control they, as an audience, have over what they consume. This worksheet could be developed to look at how music is used to influence people's behaviour, including its role in persuading people to consume a range of products.

Popular music 59

Most students are likely to respond to this worksheet by considering popular artists and bands producing music for their peer age group. However, there is no reason why they shouldn't be encouraged to focus on music targeted at a different and possibly older audience. Indeed, a comparison exercise would be interesting, to investigate the similar roles of promotional and marketing techniques despite the differences in detail. This topic is covered in detail on pages 153–9 of the textbook.

My music 60

Students will enjoy the opportunity to produce work based on their own musical tastes. Teachers may find it useful to develop the worksheet to look at the concept of segmentation, and how the mass audience for music has been broken down into smaller interest groups. The music press produces charts of individual music genres which can be used as the basis for discussion or further work in this area. Different musical styles are considered on pages 146–7 of the textbook.

Promoting a new band 61

This worksheet supports pages 153–4 of the texbook. The production opportunities can be developed to encompass designing CD and tape covers, advertisements and posters, or even mock radio interviews. Work on the music press can obviously be linked in here.

The music press 62

Worksheet 62 looks at the influence of the music press in promoting music, and gives students the chance to have a go at writing their own reviews. Teachers might like to consider using video or sound-based material as stimulus for this worksheet before giving students the opportunity to set their own agenda in choosing material for review. The music press is discussed on pages 148 and 156–7 of the textbook.

Compilation album 63

This worksheet can be developed using the work students completed on Worksheet 60 as a starting-point. Students will probably benefit from the opportunity to discuss some existing compilation albums, and to consider the type of audience these are marketed for. It will help with the design work (Task B) if some time is spent considering the design of existing CD packaging. An existing insert could be used to develop a template for the students' own design. Further work could be developed in the promotion and marketing of the CD, through, for example, TV and radio advertisements.

10. Advertising

160-173

Advertising has always been a popular area for investigation in Media Studies. Texts are readily available and easily updated, and the advertising itself takes in a range of media forms. Studying similar texts across a range of media provides students with some useful insights into the comparative codes and conventions of each context in which an advertisement may be placed. Advertising can also offer opportunities for the study of intertextuality – the way that advertisements themselves often borrow from or refer to other media forms.

Advertising record

This worksheet, which supports the 'On your own' activity on page 160 of the textbook, should help create in students an awareness of the all-pervasive nature of advertising in a media-saturated society. Students may find that using five-bar gates is the best way of filling in the grid. Teachers may like to consider getting students to present the results of their survey as a display in graphical form. The class might also like to consider if it is possible ever to avoid contact with, or being influenced by, advertisements.

Targeting adverts

This worksheet develops Worksheet 65 by considering how advertisements may be targeted at specific groups. Again there are opportunities to develop the work here, by considering what groups are most often targeted and what sort of products are aimed at them. It might also be worth tying in this work with the concepts of audience or market segmentation (see pages 50–52 and 64–65 of the textbook) and the importance of delivering specialist interest groups to advertisers (see page 205).

Advertising campaign

The work done on the first two worksheets can be synthesised into production on Worksheet 66. It is probably not worth getting students to develop their own ideas for a product, as this can waste a lot of time on work more appropriate to packaging or even product design. The emphasis here needs to be placed on how products are promoted using the media. Teachers may also see this as an opportunity to look at the way in which many advertisements rely on stereotypes, and may like to encourage students to challenge some of those that exist.

Hidden advertising

Varieties of covert advertising are described on pages 165–166 of the textbook. Students will probably need help in identifying the nature of endorsement: this is where a media personality lends their name and support to a particular product or service. The worksheet could provide an opportunity for discussion about the ethics of covert advertising methods, as well as consideration of why these methods are so popular.

Controlling advertising

The issue of ethics and the various regulation frameworks is covered on pages 172–3 of the textbook. These pages also supply the answers to Task A (1: Independent Television Commission, 2: Radio Authority, 3–5: ASA). Teachers may like to access up-to-date information and recent decisions by the regulatory bodies through the websites that most of them now have (see Contacts and resources, pp. 127–8). It is usually possible to be included on their mailing lists. Teachers may wish to consider replacing the fictitious advertisement given here with a real case, if one is available at the time the work on advertising is done.

11. Radio

174-191

Radio can easily become a forgotten medium in Media Studies. There is a tendency to take it for granted, perhaps because it does not demand our attention in quite the same way as television and other media. Teachers who do take the time and trouble to introduce students to work on radio, however, usually find it especially rewarding. This is partly because many students have a narrow perception of radio as a purveyor of popular music, rather than as a medium with a much broader based audience appeal.

The first two worksheets here aim to get students focused on the wide range of radio output available before synthesising this into production work in the last three worksheets.

Listening to the radio

This worksheet, which supports the 'In pairs' activity on page 176 of the textbook, encourages students to identify the variety of radio stations available in most areas. If providing access to radios or listening in class is a problem, the work can be based around listings in a magazine such as *Radio Times* or in a local newspaper. Alternatively, teachers could tape material and play this back to the students. Teachers may wish to take the opportunity to encourage students to become familiar with stations that they do not generally listen to.

Radio station profile (70)

This worksheet asks students to give a profile of a specific station. This may be their own favourite station, or you may again wish to encourage them to engage with radio output that they might not normally listen to. This work will require some protracted research at different times of day and night, and so needs careful planning and timing to be most effective. As scheduling obviously varies according to the time of day or night, it is a good idea to ask students to do some of this research as homework in the evening and at weekends. Teachers may like to consider recording on to audio tape sample output from particular stations to use as an exemplar to help prepare students for their own research. This worksheet supports the 'Radio station profile' activity on page 178 of the textbook.

A new station 1–3 (71)(72)(73)

These worksheets provide a series of interlinked activities surrounding the design and marketing of a new radio station which will broadcast to the local community. They readily lend themselves to group activities. Where teachers feel it is appropriate, some of the activities may be developed beyond the pre-production stage to include fully realised pieces of production work. For example jingles, slogans and logos can all actually be made, using fairly basic equipment and skills. Teachers wishing to do so might also offer students the opportunity to record segments of the pilot show on Worksheet 75. Where such realised productions are achieved, it may be worth considering whether this work might form the basis for the practical production required in Section B of the coursework folder (SEG). The identity of radio stations and the content of programmes are discussed on pages 183–9 of the textbook; page 197 touches on radio commercials.

12. Television news

192-203

While teachers may have found that a topic such as soaps has an immediate appeal with students, the opposite may well be true with TV news: teachers are likely to find initial resistance from students to the topic. This can, however, have certain advantages, not least the fact that it can be studied with greater objectivity than those genres which may be more popular with young people.

Types of TV news (74)

Worksheet 74 introduces the idea of different types of news, an important issue which is touched on in various contexts throughout chapter 12 of the textbook. Again it may be useful to modify some of the categories in light of the content of the chosen bulletin. Question C can be used as a starting-point for work on news sources, particularly to explore the extent to which news agendas are often predetermined because coverage has been planned in advance.

News coverage on TV (75)

Worksheet 75 serves to identify the importance of news as part of the scheduling of terrestrial, cable and satellite channels. Page 193 of the textbook is particularly relevant reading. By looking at how news programmes fit into TV news stations' schedules, students may be asked to consider the role of news particularly in relation to prime-time viewing, and to consider the pressure on producers to deliver news that fits in with the need for entertainment. Get each group to calculate a different day's news coverage, making sure that weekends are covered and can be compared with weekdays. The whole class can fill in the middle column of the table; those who finish quickly can then move on to calculate the percentages in the right-hand column. (Calculators will be useful for this task.)

Students could present their information as a bar chart, with the 24-hour clock along the bottom and the number of minutes of news coverage along the vertical axis. Each channel could be represented by a different colour within each bar. This would highlight competition between channels, and times of day when news programmes tend to be scheduled, such as breakfast, lunchtime and early evening. Reasons for this scheduling could be discussed.

A close look at a news story (76)

This worksheet should be used to get students to look in detail at a specific story. Careful guidance will be needed to ensure that an appropriate story is chosen. Teachers will find it useful to work through an example in class before asking students to undertake their own analysis.

TV news running order (77)

The running order is decribed on pages 197–198 of the textbook. Before answering Task B, students may find it useful to read the section on news values on page 118 of the textbook. The simulation in Worksheet 77 can obviously be modified and updated as necessary. Teachers may like to consider the value of adapting the worksheet to look at two bulletins, each aimed at a different audience. You could also provide students with a template of a running list to fill in, or adapt the production sheet (Worksheet 82). Group activities developed from this worksheet might include a role-play based on the idea of a news conference held to discuss these stories. The worksheet would then support the 'In groups' activity on page 203 of the textbook.

Writing a news script (78)

This scripting exercise could be written for a family audience as well as a youth one. The production sheet (Worksheet 82) or storyboard sheet (Worksheet 9) can be used for this. Teachers may like to consider imposing a time-limit for the item so that students will have to work within this constraint and prioritise and select the material as appropriate. With slight modification and some imagination, this might also be realised as a finished piece of video production work. The techniques of writing a news script are discussed on pages 197–198 in the textbook.

13. Practical production and assignments

Practical production

An important decision teachers need to take at an early stage is exactly how prescriptive to be in determining what productions students are to undertake.

One approach to the practical production is to introduce students to a range of production facilities, and then allow them a free choice of the medium in which they wish to work. This is obviously a resource-intensive and time-consuming approach, and most teachers will wish to limit the range of options available to their students.

At the other end of the spectrum is the highly prescriptive approach which directs all students to produce, say, a magazine cover, contents page and inside feature. Some teachers go further and determine the proposed market, for example a unisex teen magazine. Often this approach is forced upon teachers by a lack of access to production resources within a school or college. While it provides a greater degree of structure and control, there is a danger that creativity will be inhibited.

Teachers who opt for this latter strategy will do best to give students as much freedom of choice as they can within the parameters they feel obliged to set. For example, a wide range of options in terms of potential markets may help students focus more fully on the needs of their audience. In fact, peer group audiences often lead students to make assumptions without fully investigating the potential of the market.

Sometimes, where production facilities are limited, students may ask to use their own, for example home computers or the family's video camera. Whilst this is acceptable, teachers need to be confident that students are producing their own work and not relying on family or friends to do this. Both the teacher and candidate are required to sign an authentication and to acknowledge any help from outside sources on the Candidate Assessment Sheet.

Group work is a further issue that teachers may have to address. This is an attractive option, both because it eases pressure on production resources and because it reflects normal working practice in most media industries. Many group productions work well, with students producing sophisticated and imaginative responses; others end in failure, with little or nothing to show for their efforts. The composition of groups needs careful consideration, as does their size (four is the maximum number advised).

Teachers should also bear in mind when assessing group work that individual contribution to the production should be identified and rewarded in the final assessment. This can probably be best achieved by ensuring that the students have clearly defined individual roles and responsibilities within the group. Students should also be reminded that even where a production is created by a group, each member is required to produce an individual supporting account.

Timing is also a key factor. In general, production work will take longer than is anticipated. Careful planning at an early stage can help avoid some of the bottlenecks that are likely to occur when all students are wanting to get access to the same piece of equipment simultaneously. Teachers should encourage forward thinking not only in order to maximise access to scarce production facilities, but also so that students are aware of the number of activities and tasks that their production involves, and how long each will take.

Production planning sheets (79) (80) (81a) (81b) (81c)

The production planning sheets should be used as an initial focus for students to think through their strategy for work on their production. They can also be photocopied as a record of the student's original intent, as students often stray from their initial brief towards a wholly different production. This is particularly true of group production work, which teachers will need to steer even more carefully. This record of original intent can be used in the student's supporting account.

Worksheet 79 uses the headings on pages 204–7 of the textbook to organise the planning sheet. It will also give some indication of the demand that is likely to be made on resources, to enable the teacher to make necessary plans to ensure adequate access for all students. It also provides an opportunity to encourage students to undertake realistic and achievable productions. Over-ambition at this stage can lead to a lot of disappointment later.

Worksheet 80 reinforces the link between production practice and the key concepts of Media Studies. In this way, students will be reminded of the close ties between theory and practice, and will relate these in their production, rather than seeing production as an end in itself.

Worksheets 81a–c are designed to provide students with both a framework and a checklist to guide them through the stages of production. Three separate worksheets have been provided, which should cover most video, sound and print productions respectively. The worksheets should encourage students to undertake the production tasks in a logical order, and to ensure that each stage is completed before the next is undertaken. Working in an orderly and logical way can help prevent students wasting time, as well as maximise the use of scarce production resources and equipment.

Production sheet;
Shot list; Log sheet for video; Editing sheet;
Design sheet for magazine/
newspaper **82** **83** **84** **85** **86**

These worksheets enable a variety of planning and scripting tasks to be undertaken as central parts of the production. Worksheet 9 can be used as a storyboard template. Teachers should emphasise to the students the importance of keeping such materials. Where appropriate, these can be submitted as part of the final production. Evidence of audience surveys, research into the specific topic, scripts and storyboards is particularly helpful to the moderator.

Production diary **87**

Students will need one worksheet for each session of production work they undertake. The production diary will provide a useful record for students of the work they have planned and undertaken. Students should be encouraged to complete their diary at the end of each session of work on the practical production. The record of decisions that they have made will provide useful material when writing their supporting account.

Thinking about
the supporting account **88**

The use of headings in this worksheet to signal and signpost appropriate commentary helps to ensure that students focus their thoughts and produce a coherent and logical supporting account. The worksheet is intended to provide a useful link between production work and media theory. Establishing such a link is vital to the supporting account, where students are presented with an opportunity to demonstrate their grasp of theory in relation to production work. The organisation of the worksheet reflects the organisation of the account itself suggested on pages 219–225 of the textbook.

Presentation checklist **89**

This worksheet encourages students to take responsibility for organising and presenting their work – both the production and the supporting account – to its best advantage. This is especially significant where a sample has to be sent to an external moderator.

Assignments

226-229

The great benefit offered by the coursework component of a Media Studies syllabus is the freedom centres have to devise their own assessments. This section, therefore, outlines an assessment strategy for Section A of Paper 1 which should help teachers avoid some of the pitfalls associated with this part of the syllabus.

Teachers should bear in mind the syllabus requirements for Section A of Paper 1. These are the need for candidates' folders to:

1. contain three assignments of equal weighting, each of 700–800 words or the equivalent in design and production work;
2. cover all three assessment objectives (1 knowledge and understanding; 2 analysis and interpretation; 3 production skills) in the ratio of 1:2:2;
3. show evidence of engagement with the four key concepts (language, representation, institutions and audience);
4. focus on three different media.

All three assignments, each of about 700–800 words or equivalent, should then be marked together out of 60. Many teachers will, of course, expect their students to produce more than three assignments, and then to choose the highest scoring three for formal assessment.

An important change introduced in the 2003 specification is that each individual assignment must now cover all three assessment objectives. This means that as well as containing theoretical work, each one must have an element of production skills. The diagram below shows the weightings for each of the objectives within the assignment.

Assessment objectives:
1 Knowledge and understanding 20%
2 Analysis and interpretation 40%
3 Production skills 40%

This approach brings with it the advantage of integrating theoretical and practical elements in the same way as is required by both production work in Section B and the Controlled Test. Students, therefore, should be comfortable with an integrated approach to theory and production from an early stage in their course.

Another issue that teachers need to take on board is the importance of keeping assignment work within the 700–800 words or equivalent limit required by the syllabus. Inevitably, there is a temptation to feel that if a student has worked hard and produced a lot of material, it is in some way unfair to not to assess all of it.

Of course, students may generate a good deal of background notes and response material during the course of working on a particular topic. For example, a term's work on television advertising might include:

- detailed analysis of the construction of a range of advertisements;
- investigation into the constraints under which advertisers and television companies work;
- consideration of the relationship between scheduling and the placing of advertisements, including the cost of advertising at specific times on specific channels;
- work on representation, for example on the way in which women, families or young people are represented in advertisements;
- examination of audience research and the composition of audiences, with the possibility of work on media effects;
- the production of students' own advertisements, either as storyboard/script or even as video productions.

The assignment that emerges from this work cannot hope to cover all of these areas in 700–800 words. The teacher, however, needs to design an assignment brief which will provide the student with an opportunity to demonstrate the understanding and analytical and production skills that they have developed in exploring the topic.

Assignment brief   **90**

Worksheet 90 offers an example of the type of assignment that can most effectively be set. It begins with textual analysis, through the deconstruction of an existing advertisement. Here students are asked to choose their own, but teachers will obviously need to provide guidance.

The assignment then prompts the student to explore the key concept of representation. However, it would be easy at this point to substitute another key concept, for example, institutions. This might take the form of a task based on the regulation of advertising.

Assessment objective 3 is covered by means of synthesising the work into production skills in the form of a storyboard and magazine advertisement. Of course, this could equally take the form of video work, possibly as a group activity. On this worksheet, the production work is based on representation, but if institutions were the key concept being explored, it might have been in the form of scripting an advertisement that offended some aspect of the Advertising Standards Agency (ASA) code.

The final task is an evaluative one, requiring the student to consider their own product in relation to the conventions of the mainstream media.

Not only does shaping the assignment in the way indicated make the assessment of the coursework folder much simpler, students should benefit from an integrated approach to the teaching and assessment of a topic.

This approach may usefully be summarised as follows:

Textual analysis → Development of a key concept → Production → Evaluation

It can be used as a template for the exploration of a range of forms and genres. For example, the starting point might be magazine covers. These texts could then be explored in terms of audience as the key concept, with students producing their own magazine cover targeted at specific audiences.

Media texts make a useful and logical starting point for much assignment work. However, where teachers wish to vary the approach, it is simply a matter of choosing a different starting point. For example, they may consider the representation of families in TV advertising in general terms and then focus the assignment down to a specific text. Equally in the second example, the regulation of the advertising industry, for example, through the work of the ASA, might be used as the initial stimulus.

As with all Media Studies work, much will depend on the interests, abilities and motivation of the class.

14. The Controlled Test

Student's Book   230-238

A key decision for the teacher is how much preparation time to spend on the controlled test topic, and when this work should be done. Students are issued with the test on 1 May and take it under exam conditions in sessions totalling three hours during May.

Many centres find that the best time to introduce work on the topic is in the term immediately preceding the test. This ensures that the topic is fresh in students' minds as they go into the test. Consideration should, however, be given to introducing this work much earlier in the course, possibly as early as the last term of the first year on a two-year course. This allows students the opportunity to spend most of their second year immersing themselves in the topic, by ensuring that they look at a range of relevant texts, and by collecting and researching appropriate materials.

Another advantage of this is that the teacher is able to make the topic a reference point throughout the year as other areas of the syllabus are discussed and worked on. An introductory session of between four and six weeks of a couple of hours per week can then be supported by a period of revision just before the end of the fifth term.

Most of the tasks that students attempt as part of their course can be seen in some way as preparation for the controlled test. The following worksheets, however, serve to highlight some of the specific skills and knowledge that they may need to apply in completing the test. The worksheets are split into two groups; Worksheets 91–95 are designed to help with long-term preparation for the test, while Worksheets 96–101 are intended for students to use when the paper has been issued.

Researching around the topic **91**

Teachers will have their individual strategies for approaching the topic area and deciding how teaching it should fit into their scheme of work. If, however, the topic is introduced reasonably early in the course, this will give students the opportunity to research it over a sustained period. Worksheet 94 offers ideas for the kind of research activity that can serve as useful preparation. Many of these activities lend themselves to group work.

The key concepts **92**

Confidence in applying the key concepts is often the recipe for success in GCSE Media Studies work. Worksheet 92 serves to remind students of the importance of these in relation to the Controlled Test, and encourages students to make them a guiding principle in their approach to the topic.

Storyboard practice **93**

Students will each need two storyboard sheets (use Worksheet 9 for this task). Worksheet 93 revisits the analysis of a moving image and seeks to reinforce confidence in handling storyboard techniques. Particularly important is encouraging students to use the correct terminology, for example in describing the size of shot or type of edit. In choosing material for analysis, teachers should bear in mind that the sequence must have a variety of shots and edit techniques, and a soundtrack. It may be necessary to show the chosen sequence several times. A video playback with a real-time counter or a stopwatch are useful to obtain precise timings.

Using a production sheet (TV) **94**

A similar activity is offered in Worksheet 94, this time using the production sheet (Worksheet 82). Teachers may wish to use the same TV sequence or introduce a new one. By practising these two approaches to scripting – storyboard and production sheet – students have an opportunity to decide which is likely to be the more effective approach for them, especially where they may feel compromised by their lack of drawing skills. Students will each need two copies of Worksheet 82 for this task.

Using a production sheet (radio) **95**

Worksheet 95 develops scripting skills further in terms of radio work. Again teachers need to make a careful choice of sequence to ensure that an appropriate variety of techniques are employed for scripting.

Designing a poster or advertisement **96**

Worksheet 96 reinforces earlier work on image analysis and seeks to give students confidence in design and layout skills.

Preparing to tackle the questions;
Preparation checklist;
Timing the test **97** **98** **99**

Worksheets 97 and 98 are intended to get students focused on their approach to the controlled test tasks. Timing, as in all exams, is an important issue: Worksheet 99, therefore, will help students to calculate the amount of time it is appropriate to spend on each task.

Practising your presentation skills **100**

There is a tendency among students to go into essay writing mode as soon as the word examination is mentioned. Worksheet 100 attempts to get students to consider how they can use their presentation skills to enhance their responses to in-role tasks. This worksheet develops material on page 230–231 of the textbook.

Test schedule and checklists **101**

Worksheet 101 will help candidates to ensure that they arrive at the right place at the right time, with the right equipment. Simply remembering to bring colouring materials to the exam room can considerably enhance the quality and effectiveness of storyboard and designs. The worksheet also includes a checklist to be memorised for the last session of the test: in the midst of the euphoria of completing the test, it is useful for students to be reminded to check through their script to make sure it is as accurate and examiner-friendly as possible. This part of the worksheet reinforces the advice on page 238 of the textbook.

You and the media

A Tick each product that you consider to be a part of the mass media:

- ☐ Television news
- ☐ Women's magazines
- ☐ School or college prospectus
- ☐ Computer game
- ☐ Radio phone-in
- ☐ Billboard advert
- ☐ DVD from the rental shop
- ☐ Exhibition of photographs
- ☐ Shakespeare play at the local theatre
- ☐ BBC Online website

B By considering your answers to the above, give two important characteristics that mass media products have in common.

1. ....

2. ....

C Name one mass media product that you consume regularly (at least once a week).

....

Why do you use it? ....

....

D Is there any media product that you feel you could not live without? If so, say what it is and why it is so important to you.

....

....

....

....

E How do you think that the media influences the way in which you live your life? Give some examples of this.

....

....

....

....

How different people view the media

A In the grid below, write the name of someone you know opposite each of the descriptions. You will need to ask the person you name to fill in a questionnaire, so make sure it is someone you can get in touch with easily.

Description	Name
A person of your age, but the opposite sex	
A man drawing a pension	
A woman drawing a pension	
A woman who has a professional job (e.g. teacher, lawyer, doctor)	
A person with disability (e.g. hearing or sight impairment, or using a wheelchair)	
A person who spends time at home looking after children	
A man or woman from an ethnic minority group (e.g. Asian, Afro-Caribbean, Chinese)	
A man with a manual job (e.g. a joiner, driver, builder)	

B Now you need to construct a questionnaire about how they use the media. Think about these issues when you are wording your questions:

- Which media do they most frequently use – radio, print, music, computer, television, the internet?
- Which of those media do they use the most?
- What do they look forward to the most in the media?
- Do they feel that the media influences their lives? If so, how?
- Do they feel there are too many media products in today's society?
- What aspect of the media plays the biggest part in their life?

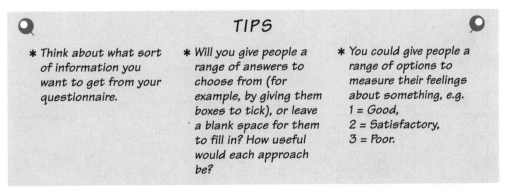

TIPS

* Think about what sort of information you want to get from your questionnaire.

* Will you give people a range of answers to choose from (for example, by giving them boxes to tick), or leave a blank space for them to fill in? How useful would each approach be?

* You could give people a range of options to measure their feelings about something, e.g. 1 = Good, 2 = Satisfactory, 3 = Poor.

Media Studies for GCSE Teaching Pack

Diary of media consumption

Student's Book 2-7

In the chart below, fill in the details of what you consume over three days and the amount of time you spend consuming it. Don't forget that listening to the radio or music while travelling in a car or on public transport, or even walking along, counts.

	Print		TV		Radio		Music (tapes, CDs)		The Internet	
	■ item	■ time	■ item	■ time	■ item	■ time	■ item	■ time	■ item	■ time
Day 1										
Day 2										
Day 3										
TOTAL										

Image analysis

Look carefully at the image you have been given and answer the following questions.

A Describe what you see when you look at the image.

....

....

....

B What do you think the purpose of the image is (e.g. to sell or to inform)?

Purpose ....

C Now look very carefully at the image and write down what you see in relation to the following headings.

LOOK AT	WHAT YOU SEE
Size	
Type of shot (LS etc.)	
Angle	
Setting	
Framing	
Focus	
Colour	
Lighting	
Pose	
Composition	
Subject matter, including people	
Text	

D What is your personal response to the image? Do you like or dislike it? Explain why.

....

....

....

E Consider the connotations of the image. What do you think the image is designed to make you feel? How does it have this effect?

....

....

Anchorage

Captions

Look at the image that your teacher has given you. Its caption has been removed.

 A Discuss what you think the original caption was. List three possibilities below.

1. ....

2. ....

3. ....

 B Share your captions. Discuss:

1. How much can you change the meaning by adding your own caption?

2. Is it possible to make a serious image appear comic?

3. Do you think newspapers and magazines ever set out deliberately to change the meaning of an image by the caption they use?

Look through newspapers and magazines to try to find examples of images where the meaning has been interpreted by a caption.

Cropping

C Another way to change the meaning of an image is to 'crop' it. Cover up certain areas of the image using a sheet of blank paper cut into shape and see how you can change its meaning.

D Produce a new caption for the cropped image.

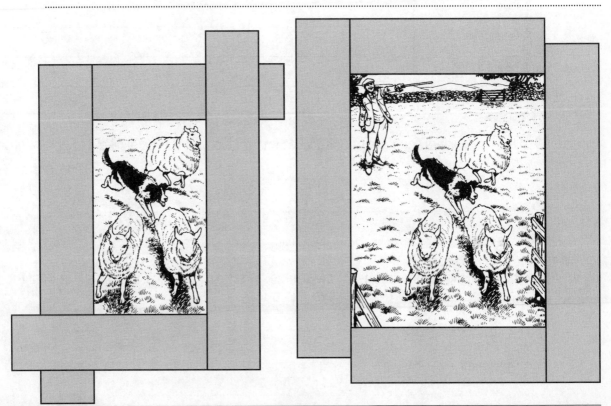

Codes

 A Take a simple sentence and put it into code. Now see if the rest of the class can discover what it means.

 B Look at the weather chart on page 17 of the textbook. Copy eight of the symbols used into the chart below and write alongside what each symbol means. Explain briefly how you know what it means.

Symbol	Meaning	How do you know?
1.		
2.		
3.		
4.		
5.		
6.		
7.		
8.		

 C Discuss why you think a weather chart is an example of a code. List some of the other codes that you know.

 D Watch an extract from a television programme with the sound mute. Decide what type of programme it is. Make a list of the visual features that help you decide what type of programme it is.

E People whose hearing is impaired may not be able to decode the sound element of television's message. How can this be overcome? How does the media give information about the world to people whose sight is impaired?

Reading the media

A Choose a full-page magazine advertisement that interests you or is particularly striking in its impact on you. Make sure it contains words as well as images.

Name of product ....

B Describe briefly the context in which you found it, e.g. an upmarket women's magazine or a tabloid newspaper.

Context ....

....

C By paying particular attention to the visual images in the advertisement and the way in which these link to the written words, write a paragraph explaining how you 'read' the advertisement. You may find it useful to consider some of these factors:

- Colour
- Framing
- Composition
- Size
- Type of shot
- Subject matter, including people
- Setting
- Lighting
- Pose
- Text.

D Think about the connotations that you find in the images.

1. Do you find these appealing?

2. How do you feel they will appeal to other people, of different ages and gender?

3. How do the images relate to the product that is being sold?

E You will hear the expression that people are said to be 'reading the media'. Talk about why you think the expression 'reading' is used here, when you usually associate it with written words.

Analysing moving images

A Watch carefully the television sequence that your teacher shows you. In the boxes provided, sketch a shot that you have seen that fits in with the description above the box. Underneath, explain briefly why you think this shot was chosen, and what effect it will have on the viewer.

Long shot (LS)

Medium shot (MS)

....

....

....

....

....

Close up (CU)

Big close up (BCU)

....

....

....

....

B Now watch the same sequence again, and fill in the table below. This time you should concentrate on the way in which the camera is used. Give one example of each type of shot or camera movement.

Type of shot/ movement	Brief details	Why chosen/effect
Pan		
Tilt		
High-angle shot		
Low-angle shot		
Shot where the camera is canted (not horizontal)		
Zoom		
Point of view shot		

C Now do the same thing, this time looking for different types of edit. When filling in the third column, think about what edits tell us about the passage of time.

Type of edit	Brief details	Why chosen/effect
Cut		
Fade		
Dissolve		
Wipe		

D Using a stopwatch, or the counter on a video player or edit suite, note the length of time the first four sequences run between edits.

Sequence no.	Brief details	Timing (seconds)
1		
2		
3		
4		

Are you surprised by the length of time in each case? Why do you think it is different for each sequence?

Advert storyboard

Using this sheet, construct a storyboard for a TV advertisement. Remember that a good storyboard will usually include a variety of different shots.

Timing (seconds)		Shot/camera movement	Sound (dialogue/ music/sound effects)
	Edit:		
	Edit:		
	Edit:		
	Edit:		
	Edit:		

Narrative

A Choose any of the following media texts:

- a TV advert
- a radio news bulletin
- a tabloid news story
- a film/TV drama.

Identify the main characters.

....

....

B Carefully looking at your media text, try to break down the narrative to fit in with the categories in the boxes below.

What is the opening situation? (How does the story start?)	
What is the problem or challenge that is posed?	
How does this create conflict between characters?	
How is this resolved?	
How is the closing situation different to the opening situation? What has changed?	

C Do we see the story from one character's point of view? How is this acheived?

....

....

Narrative and genre

Imagine the following situation:

● Boy arranges to meet girl outside the cinema at 7.30 p.m.

● Girl arrives early and waits.

● Boy is walking through the park to the cinema, when he is abducted by alien life forms.

● Girl gets tired of waiting and goes home.

For each of the following genres, describe how you think the story would be told, identifying its key features and style.

1. Television news

....

....

....

....

2. Sitcom

....

....

....

....

3. Pop video

....

....

....

....

4. Problem page of teen magazine

....

....

....

....

 B Choose one of these genres and write the script or text of the story.

Icons

Student's Book 8-29

A Films shown at the cinema or on television are often described as belonging to a particular category. Use the chart below to match the images (or icons) that you might see in a film to one or more of the types of film listed on the left. For example, if you think icons 9 and 11 are found in detective films, write 9 and 11 in the first box. Remember that some icons may appear in more than one genre.

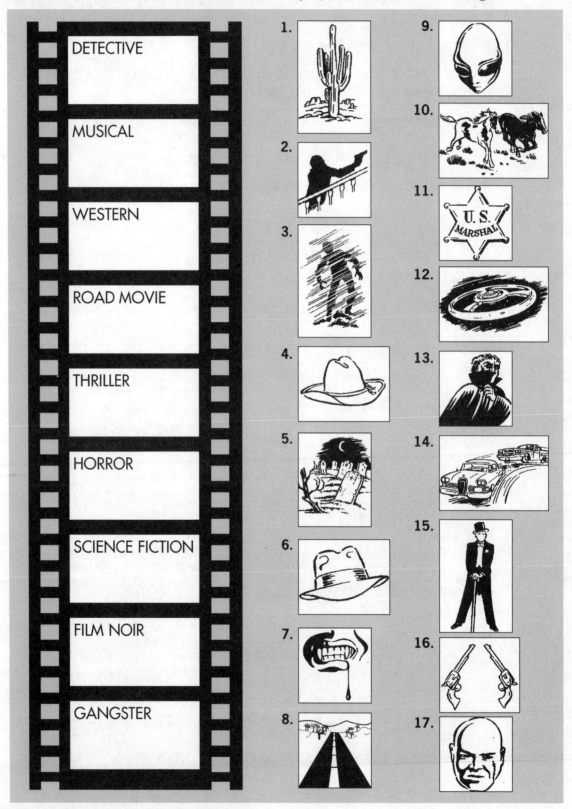

DETECTIVE

MUSICAL

WESTERN

ROAD MOVIE

THRILLER

HORROR

SCIENCE FICTION

FILM NOIR

GANGSTER

1.
2.
3.
4.
5.
6.
7.
8.
9.
10.
11. U.S. MARSHAL
12.
13.
14.
15.
16.
17.

B Why do you think that certain images are used over and over again in films of a particular genre?

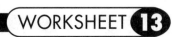

Sitcom analysis

Choose any situation comedy that you have watched on television or heard on the radio. Analyse an episode and complete the chart. If you have seen or heard other episodes, you can include information from them too.

Name of show:	
Situation	
Location	
Is it typical of the genre?	
Commonly used narrative (typical storylines)	
Themes (ideas that keep recurring e.g. the problem of having teenage children)	
Main source of comedy; how does this relate to the themes?	
Schedule (channel and time)	
Audience appeal (why is the programme popular?)	

Sitcom characters

Using the same programme that you considered in Worksheet 13, analyse the types of characters by completing the tasks below.

A List three of the main characters. Identify their main characteristics.

1. Name of character: ....

Main characteristics: ....

....

....

2. Name of character: ....

Main characteristics: ....

....

....

3. Name of character: ....

Main characteristics: ....

....

....

B Are there other types of characters? Fill in the grid below for two other characters.

Name of character:	
Young/old	Male/female
Personality traits	
Section of the audience s/he appeals to	
Reasons for this	

Name of character:	
Young/old	Male/female
Personality traits	
Section of the audience s/he appeals to	
Reasons for this	

C Now try to think of a real person who fits in with the description of any of these characters.

Features of soap operas

 A Soap operas are an example of a television genre. They all have certain features in common. In the grid below, try to identify what you consider the most important of these features to be, and provide an example of each from a soap currently being shown on television.

	Feature	Example
Setting 1.	*Northern city's backstreets*	*Coronation Street*
2.		
3.		
Characters 1.		
2.		
3.		
Narrative 1.		
2.		
3.		
Social issues 1.		
2.		
3.		

B Soaps, or serial dramas as they are often called, are sometimes considered to reflect what happens in real life. As such, they are examples of realism. From the list of features you have made above, choose two that you consider are truly 'realistic' or 'unrealistic', and explain why you think this is so.

Feature 1: ....

This feature contributes to/detracts from the sense of realism created by soaps because:

....

....

....

....

Feature 2: ....

This feature contributes to/detracts from the sense of realism created by soaps because:

....

....

....

....

Representing you

You will need to find two photographs of yourself taken at roughly the same time.

- The first photograph should be one that represents you as you like the world to see you.
- The second should be a photograph that shows you as you don't like the world to see you.

A Now complete the following chart.

	Photo 1	Photo 2
Brief description of how you appear in the photo		
What do you like/ dislike about the image?		
How do you think other people will read the image?		
Do you think the image is a true representation of you?		

B Imagine the photo is to be used in your local newspaper because you have just won a competition. Write a caption for each photo.

Photo 1 ....

....

Photo 2 ....

....

Re-presentation

Your teacher will set up an event (or series of events) for you to watch. Imagine you are a reporter who has just witnessed this event.

A Take five minutes to write down quickly in note form everything that you can remember about the event.

B Using your notes, try to organise the 'story' of what happened into a sequence in which the most important information is given first.

C If you were able to have a still camera to record the event, what one picture would you most like to have taken?

D Using the materials you have got, write a story for your local newspaper that tells what happened. You should include a sketch of your imaginary picture with a caption.

E Compare your story with those produced by the rest of the class. Has everyone agreed what is the most important part of the event? Do you all have the same choice of picture? If there are differences, how do you explain these?

F Do you think some versions are more accurate than others? Give your reasons.

Techniques of representation

For this task, you will need to watch a short extract from a documentary programme or news report, and then consider some of the techniques that are used to represent the world to a television audience.

 A Explain how the **sound** element of the programme is being used to produce a particular representation. Think about:

- the voice-over or commentary
- the use of music or sound effects.

B What effect does the **camerawork** have on the portrayal? Think about:

- how the camera is positioned relative to the subject
- the size of shot (e.g. a close up)
- any camera movement.

Remember to look out for:

- the point-of-view shot, where the camera shows the audience what a particular person in the programme sees
- reaction shots, where a person's response is shown.

C What is the importance of the **editing** that has taken place? Think about:

- what has been included
- what may have been left out
- the order in which the scenes have been put together
- the devices used for linking the scenes together.

 D Do you think the extract you have seen is intended to make the audience respond in a specific way? Do you think it is possible for the audience to react in a different way?

Content analysis

For this activity you will need to look at an edition of a tabloid newspaper. You will be analysing photographs and other pictorial material containing images of females in both the editorial and advertising sections of the paper.

A Work carefully through the newspaper and examine each image in detail. Then make notes on each image under the following headings:

- Brief description
- Details of female
- Age
- Appearance
- Alone/with male/with female/in group
- Location, e.g. home, car, office
- Active/passive/neutral image
- Positive/negative/neutral image

B Now look at what you have found and answer the following questions.

1. Do women of a certain age appear more frequently than others, e.g. younger women?

....

....

2. Do women of a specific type of appearance feature more commonly? If so, which?

....

....

3. What are women seen doing most often?

....

....

4. Where are they most often seen doing it?

....

....

5. Are women featured most often with men, or with women, or alone?

....

....

 C What does the above information tell you about the way women are represented in the popular press?

Stereotypes

A What do you understand by the term 'stereotype'? Come up with a group definition.

....

....

....

....

B Discuss the following:

1. How do you think stereotypes come about?

2. Do we only create stereotypes of people we fear or distrust?

3. Do stereotypes ever have any truth in them?

C Choose a group of people that you think are often portrayed as stereotypes. Now keep a look out in the media for representations of this group of people. Keep a diary, detailing both positive and negative representations, and the time, date and programme. You should also collect cuttings of images of that group.

After a week, sort your diary notes and clippings into these categories:

- positive
- negative
- neutral.

D On balance, how would you say the media has represented this group of people?

....

....

....

....

....

E Does this tell you anything about what our society thinks of these people?

....

....

....

....

....

Are you a stereotype?

A Are you a stereotype? Consider the different groups in society that you can be associated with. You might like to think in terms of:

- age
- gender
- social background
- where you live
- hobbies and interests (e.g. sport or musical tastes).

List the groups to which you belong in the first column of the table below.

Now list, in the second column of the table, what you think are likely to be the stereotypical features of each group. (Note there could be several different features for each group.)

In the third column, indicate which features you think accurately represent the way you are, and which you think are inaccurate. An example has been given to start you off.

Groups to which I belong	Stereotypical features	Accurate or not?
Teenagers	*1. Spotty* *2. Moody adolescent*	*No!* *Sometimes*

B What does this tell you about stereotypes? Think about:

- how your own attitude to these groups is affected by stereotypes;
- how society as a whole values these groups;
- how much responsibility the media has for how these groups are treated by society.

Positive and negative representations

Using either the examples you worked on in Worksheets 18–20, or another group of your choosing that you feel is generally given negative representation, have a go at the following tasks.

A Using the table below, list what characteristics of the group are represented in a negative way. Next to this, make a list of positive characteristics that could be used to represent the people in the group.

Name of group:	
Negative characteristics	**Positive characteristics**

B Using your list, create a storyboard for a TV ad or programme trail that presents a positive image of the group.

C After you have created your storyboard, describe some of the difficulties you encountered in creating a positive representation. Explain how you tried to overcome these difficulties.

Institutions

A Below is a list of media products that are produced by media institutions. Complete the chart by first of all providing an example of one of these products. Next find out which organisation made the product, and put its name in the last column.

TYPE OF PRODUCT	NAME OF PRODUCT	PRODUCED BY
TV SITCOM		
CHILDREN'S COMIC		
WOMEN'S MAGAZINE		
BROADSHEET NEWSPAPER		
LOCAL RADIO STATION		
COMPUTER GAME		
WILDLIFE PROGRAMME ON TV		
FILM AVAILABLE AS VIDEO RENTAL		

B Share your findings and answer the following questions together.

1. Which of the company names do you recognise?

....

....

....

2. Are certain production companies associated with particular genres of programmes?

....

....

Ownership

Student's Book 42-57

Large media organisations are usually public companies, which means they are owned by shareholders, all of whom have individual shares. These shares can be bought and sold on the stock exchange. Find a newspaper which lists share prices under various headings, and look at the companies listed under the heading 'media'.

A How many of the listed companies do you recognise, from your own consumption of the media?

....

....

....

B News International is an example of a multinational company with a wide range of media interests, such as TV stations and newspapers. For each of the media listed in the table below, give the name of one of New International's interests in the UK, the USA and Australia.

	UK	USA	Australia
Newspapers			
Television			
Music/radio			

C Do you think the public should be concerned that one company has so many media interests? Give your reasons.

....

....

....

....

....

Alternative media

Student's Book 42-57

Not all media institutions are large public companies. In fact some are much more informal organisations, run by individuals or groups of people. They are sometimes called 'alternative media'.

A What do you think this name implies?

....

....

B Can you think of any examples of alternative media? (You might like to think about fanzines or websites produced by fans for football clubs or pop bands.) How do people get to see these products? Do you or your friends consume any of them?

....

....

....

....

....

....

C Imagine that you decide to set up a fanzine or website for a local sports club or pop band. Describe briefly what you think should be included in it.

....

....

....

....

....

....

D Explain briefly how your magazine or website will appeal to the audience in a way that a mainstream publication would not. Outline how and where you would distribute your fanzine or publicise your website.

....

....

....

....

....

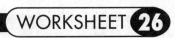

Job adverts

A For this worksheet you will need two advertisements for jobs in the media. Make sure they are for different media, for example one from television and one from the print media. Complete the grid below, using the information you have found in both advertisements.

	Job 1	Job 2
Job title		
Medium		
Institution		
Location		
Salary		
Experience needed		
Qualities required		
Personal characteristics		
Educational background		
Duties		

B Which aspects of these jobs are similar and which are different? How do you account for these differences?

C What conclusions can you draw about the type of person that media institutions want to employ? What does this tell you about the values of the institutions themselves?

Applying for a job

Choose one of the jobs that you analysed in Worksheet 26. Fill in the following application form for the job, inventing any details you think would be necessary to give you a chance of getting it. Remember that presentation is important on an application form: write neatly and clearly or use a word processor.

APPLICATION FORM

■ Name

■ Education

■ Age

■ Current position and previous experience

■ Hobbies and interests

■ Explain in no more than 100 words why you think you are suitable for this job

Student's Book 42-57

Newsreaders and reporters

Watch the evening news bulletins on BBC 1, ITV and Channel 5. Use the table below to make notes about the newsreaders and reporters.

	BBC 1	ITV	Channel 5
■ How do they dress?			
■ How do they speak (accent/use of words)?			
■ How do they address the audience?			
■ How do they make their report, or read their story?			

Costing a video film

Student's Book 42-57

A Imagine that you have been asked by a local cable TV company to make a short documentary about a typical week in the life of your class. The film is to be broadcast to the local community using one of their cable channels.

Use the table below to make a list of what you think you would need to complete the production. (An example has been given to start you off.) Remember that you will need equipment for filming, such as cameras, recorders, microphones, tripods and lighting. Your teacher will supply you with some details of the cost of hiring equipment locally. You will also need time working in an editing suite, and you may wish to use a professional presenter to add a voice-over, together with some appropriate music. You may decide to use technical staff who are skilled in operating all the equipment; if so, they will need to be paid.

Calculate the total cost of your documentary and the total time it will take to make. Then fill in the bottom line of the table.

Item	Daily/hourly rate	Time required	Cost
1. Edit suite	£150 per day	2 days	£300
2.			
3.			
4.			
5.			
6.			
7.			
8.			
9.			
TOTAL			

B Once you have costed out the production, make a list of the places where you might go to raise the money for this venture.

Popularity and success

A Here is some research for you to do. What is:

1. the most popular programme currently showing on all terrestrial TV channels

2. the most popular programme on BBC 2

3. the newspaper that sells the most copies on weekdays

4. the number of copies the *Daily Telegraph* usually sells each day

5. the programme most people watch on Satellite and Cable TV

6. the best-selling music album of all time

7. the most popular film currently showing at the cinema

8. the most popular video for people to rent?

B 1. Which organisations are responsible for collecting this information?

2. Why do you think these figures are collected?

3. To whom do you think they are most important?

C Discuss these questions:

1. What do you think makes these media products so popular with the audience?

2. What factors determine whether a product is likely to be successful or not?

D Choose one product from any medium and explain why you think it is so popular.

Student's Book 42-57

Scheduling

How do TV companies try to ensure that their programmes get the maximum share of the audience?

BBC 1
5.15 **NEWS AND WEATHER**
5.25 **REGIONAL NEWS AND SPORT**
5.30 **'ALLO 'ALLO**
6.00 **JIM DAVIDSON'S GENERATION GAME**
7.00 **LENNY GOES TO TOWN** In Dundee, with Mick Hucknall, Jerry Hall and Marie Helvin.
7.40 **THE NATIONAL LOTTERY DRAW**
8.05 **AIRPORT** Resident press men Steve and Russell play cat and mouse with the Spice Girls. *FILM*
9.25 **THE X FILES**
10.10 **NEWS AND WEATHER**
10.30 **NATIONAL LAMPOON'S LOADED WEAPON** (Gene Quintano, 1993) Lacklustre Lethal Weapon parody with Emilio Estevez and Samuel L. Jackson.

BBC 2
5.15 **TOTP2**
6.00 **BLUE PETER NIGHT FOR KIDS**
6.05 **CARRY ON BLUE PETER** Out-takes, live faux pas and pet antics.
6.25 **IT'S A DOG'S LIFE** Petra, Patch, Shep, Goldie et al.
7.00 **NEWS AND SPORT**
7.15 **CHRIS PATTEN'S EAST AND WEST**
7.55 **WHAT THE PAPERS SAY**
8.05 **COLD WAR** Berlin 1948-9.
8.55 **BLUE PETER NIGHT** Valerie Singleton, John Noakes and Peter Purves reunite for the first time in 27 years for an evening of errant pets and sticky back plastic. *PICK OF THE DAY*
9.00 **SPOOF PETER** With Lily Savage and French and Saunders.
9.20 **BP CONFIDENTIAL** Archive footage tracing Blue Peter's evolution.
10.20 **A RIGHT ROYAL REUNION** Valerie Singleton and the Princess Royal relive their visit to Kenya in 1971.
10.30 **MURDER AT TEA TIME**

ITV LWT
5.05 **LONDON WEEKEND TONIGHT**
5.25 **ITN NEWS AND RESULTS**
5.40 **GLADIATORS**
6.40 **YOU'VE BEEN FRAMED**
7.10 **THE MOMENT OF TRUTH**
8.10 **FAMILY FORTUNES** The Wynns from Knottingley pit their wits against the Nagras from Birmingham.
8.40 **ITN NEWS**
8.55 **POLICE CAMERA!, ACTION!**
9.25 **LONDON'S BURNING**
10.25 **THE BIG MATCH HIGHLIGHTS** The pick of the action from England's Euro 2000 qualifier against Bulgaria at Wembley earlier today, the first appearance on home soil for Glen Hoddle's men since the World Cup.

CHANNEL 4
5.00 **BROOKSIDE** Omnibus.
6.25 **RIGHT TO REPLY**
6.40 **LIBERTY! THE AMERICAN WAR OF INDEPENDENCE** France's hatred of the British prompts them to enter the Revolution by backing the fledgling republic.
7.40 **FOOTBALL ITALIA** Italy v Switzerland. Live coverage from Udine of the latest qualifying match for Euro 2000.
10.00 **DON'T LOOK NOW** (Nicholas Roeg, 1973) Roeg's masterly psychological thriller (based on a Daphne du Maurier story) uses Venice in winter to sinister Borgesian effect in telling a chilling tale about a church architect (Donald Sutherland) and his wife (Julie Christie) haunted by memories of their dead child. Apart from being scary and erotic, this poetic movie touches deep emotions about grief and parenthood. *FILM OF THE DAY*

CHANNEL 5
5.55 **NEWS**
6.00 **HERCULES: THE LEGENDARY JOURNEYS**
6.55 **NIGHT FEVER**
7.45 **NEWS**
8.05 **XENA: WARRIOR PRINCESS**
9.00 **ABDUCTION OF INNOCENCE** (James A. Contner, 1996) A rebellious teenager falls in with the wrong crowd and is accused of staging her own abduction in a ploy to get back at her strict father. Histrionic tosh starring Dirk Benedict. *FILM*
10.40 **THIEF** (Michael Mann 1981) A high-class thief attempts to settle down to a normal life, but the Mafia set out to scupper his dreams. James Caan, Tuesday Weld, Willie Nelson and James Belushi star. *FILM*

A Look at the listings above for the TV programmes between 5.00 p.m. and 11.00 p.m. on Saturday. Why do you think that BBC 1 often starts programmes at a different time to ITV?

B If you could only watch one channel for the evening, which channel would you choose? Give your reasons.

C Now look at the other terrestrial channels (BBC 2, Channel 4 and Channel 5).

1. What programmes do they offer in competition with the two major channels?

2. Is there evidence that they are appealing to a different audience?

D Imagine that you have been asked to provide the Saturday evening schedule for a sixth channel (called Channel 6). Using existing programmes shown at any time on the terrestrial channels, devise a Saturday evening's viewing that you feel would appeal to a family audience. Give reasons for the programmes you have chosen.

E Compare the evening viewing that each group has devised. Which channel is likely to be the most successful?

Controlling institutions

Like most organisations, the media are subject to controls that determine what they can and cannot do, in terms of publishing and broadcasting.

A Fill in the spaces below to list some of the organisations responsible for regulating the media. In the right-hand column, outline briefly what powers each of these bodies has.

MEDIA	CONTROLLING ORGANISATION	POWER
Commercial television		
Films available on video		
Newspapers		
Commercial radio		
Films shown at the cinema		
BBC radio and television		
Advertising in comics and magazines		
Satellite and cable television		

B Using your textbook, look at the code of practice that governs how newspaper reporters are expected to behave, and what newspapers can report. Now write a definition of what a code of practice is.

A code of practice is ....

....

....

....

C Do you feel that there should be more or less control over media organisations? Give your reasons.

....

....

....

....

....

....

Media profile

A Choose someone that you know well, other than yourself. (Avoid choosing a classmate who is likely to have similar tastes and interests as yourself. An older person, such as a grandparent, might be a better choice.)

Now complete the profile below, guessing where you don't know the answers, to show what media products they consume.

TELEVISION

Favourite channel

Favourite type of programme

Favourite celebrity

CINEMA/VIDEO

How often do they visit the cinema or rent videos?

What genre of film do they like the best?

PRINT

Daily newspaper

Sunday newspaper

Favourite magazine or comic

MUSIC

Favourite type of music

Favourite group

Favourite singer

RADIO

Favourite station

Favourite type of programme

Favourite presenter

COMPUTER

Do they play computer games?

Do they surf the net?

B Explain briefly how you think this profile fits in with what you know of their lifestyle.

The watershed and violence

Student's Book 58-75

A What do you understand by the term 'watershed' in relation to television schedules?

The watershed on television is ....

....

....

....

B What time do you think is an appropriate time for the watershed on television? Give your reasons.

The best time for the watershed on television is ....

because ....

....

....

....

C Does anyone in your home watch television after this time who you feel should not be doing so?

....

....

D Do you think some forms of violence shown on television are more acceptable than others? Think about violence in:

- cartoons
- comedy programmes
- drama or films
- news programmes.

E Do you think we should be concerned about the portrayal of violence towards specific groups of people – for example, women or girls?

F Should different rules about the depiction of violence apply to:

- satellite programmes
- radio
- newspapers
- the Internet?

Age-appropriate

 A Look at a recent issue of a magazine that is aimed at teenagers. Using the grid below, make a list of the features or articles that might be considered inappropriate for young people to read, and those that you think might be regarded as appropriate for young people to read. Then give your own view of what you think of the features in terms of their appropriateness.

Name of magazine:	
Features inappropriate for young people (title and page number)	My opinion
1.	
2.	
3.	
4.	
5.	
Features appropriate for young people (title and page number)	
1.	
2.	
3.	
4.	
5.	

B Do you think that any of the articles is inappropriate for students younger than yourself? List them and say why.

....

....

....

....

 C Can these magazines can be accused of encouraging young people to behave in a way that is 'wrong', or is their effect on young people's lifestyles mainly a positive one?

Student's Book 58-75

Audience participation

A What do you understand by the term 'audience participation'? Draft a definition.

Audience participation is ....

....

....

....

B Look at the list below of examples of audience participation. Which type of media do you associate each of them with? For each one, select an example of how the audience participates.

Type of audience participation	Relevant media	How audience participates
The studio guest		
Studio audiences		
Game shows		
Vox pops		
Phone-ins		
Letters		
Telephone voting		
Consumer affairs?		
Docu-soaps		
Surveillance cameras		
Reality TV		

C What do you consider to be the appeal of each kind of audience participation to:
- producers
- audiences?

Audience segmentation

A What do you understand by the term 'audience segmentation'? Explain your answer by giving examples from magazine publishing.

B Look at the listings below for some satellite channels. Choose one of the channels and explain what sort of audience it would appeal to.

PARAMOUNT COMEDY
7.00pm Sister, Sister **7.30pm** Roseanne **8.00** Grace Under Fire **8.30** Caroline In The City **9.00** Cybill **9.30** Ellen **10.00** Frasier **10.30** Cheers **11.00** Duckman **11.30** Morwenna Banks **Midnight** Late Night With David Letterman **1.00** Frasier **1.30** Cheers **2.00** Caroline In The City **2.30** Morwenna Banks **3.00** Roseanne **3.30** Cybill **4.00** Close

CHALLENGE TV
5.00pm Cross Wits **5.30pm** Challenge Prize Time **5.45pm** Family Fortunes **6.15** Challenge Prize Time **7.15** Fifteen To One **7.45** Challenge Prize Time **7.55** The Crystal Maze **9.00** Challenge Prize Time **9.15** Strike It Lucky **9.45** Challenge Prize Time **10.00** 3-2-1 **11.00** Challenge Prize Time **11.15** Through The Keyhole **11.45** Sticky Moments **12.30am** Family Late **(until 5.00am)**: Moonlighting **1.30** The Big Valley **2.30** Big Brother Jake **3.00** Sweet Justice **4.00** Blade Warriors **5.00** Screenshop **6.00** Close

HOME & LEISURE
9.00am The Joy Of Painting **9.30am** Gardeners' Diary **10.00** Grassroots **10.30** New Yankee Workshop **11.00** Screaming Reels **11.30** Hometime **Midday** Our House **12.30pm** Home Again With Bob Vila **1.00** Two's Country Cooking **1.30** Gimme Shelter **2.00** This Old House **2.30** Two's Country - Get Stuck In **3.00** Go Fishing **3.30** This Old House With Steve And Norm **4.00** Close

SKY SPORT 1
7.00am Sports Centre **7.15am** High 5 **7.45am** Survival Of The Fittest **8.15** Sports Centre **8.30** Racing News **9.00** Aerobics **9.30** V-max **10.00** Pool: Sam Int'l Pool Semi-final **11.00** Shooting: White Gold Clay Target Shooting **Midday** Aerobics **12.30pm** Cricket: Axa Life League **2.30** Survival Of The Fittest **3.00** Int'l Bowls: Australia Vs Wales **5.00** WWF **6.00** Sports Centre **6.30** Tartan Extra **7.30** Pavilion End **8.30** Football Special: Charity Shield Special **10.00** Sports Centre **10.15** Tartan Extra **11.15** Rugby League Academy **12.15am** Sports Centre **12.30am** Football Special: Charity Shield Special **2.00** Pavilion End **3.00** Sports Centre **3.15** Close

SCI-FI CHANNEL
8.00pm Quantum Leap **9.00** Babylon 5 **10.00** Film: *Automatic* (1994) Science Fiction. Stars Oliver Gruner, John Glover **11.45** Sf Scene Special **Midnight** Sightings **1.00** The Tomorrow People: Into The Unknown **1.30** Flash Gordon Conquers The Universe **2.00** Friday The 13th **3.00** Tales Of The Unexpected **3.30** Dark Shadows **4.00** Close

HISTORY CHANNEL
4.00pm Battleline Invasion Of Southern France **4.30pm** World War 1: Over There **5.00** Civil War Journal: The 54th Massachussetts **6.00** Ancient Mysteries: The Hidden City Of Petra **7.00** Unsolved Mysteries Of World War II: The Eagle & The Swastika **7.30** Unsolved Mysteries Of World War II: Hitler's Secret Weapons **8.00** Close

C Now choose another channel. Make a list of products that you think might be advertised on it.

D Explain what you think are the advantages of segmentation for:
- audiences
- advertisers.

Are there any disadvantages?

58-75

Having your say

A Think about the ways in which the audience can have a say in what the media puts out. For each of the media listed below, write down three examples of how members of the public are invited to participate in the content.

Television
satellite ITV
BBC 1
Channel 4
CABLE
BBC 2
Channel 5

1. *Points of View* ....
2. ....
3. ....

Radio
FM MW
LW

1. ....
2. ....
3. ....

Newspapers
DAILY NEWS
President Smith resigns!
NEWSDAY
SHOCK NEWS!

1. ....
2. ....
3. ....

Magazines
TEEN
bike monthly

1. ....
2. ....
3. ....

Popular Music

1. ....
2. ....
3. ....

B Now find an example of something in the media that you feel strongly about, for example a newspaper story that gives a negative impression of schools in your area.

1. What possible courses of action are open to you by way of complaint?

2. Write a letter to the appropriate person, outlining your objections.

Audience positioning

A Watch an edition of a wildlife programme. As you watch the programme, consider some of the ways in which you think the audience is likely to identify with the animals featured in the programme.

You should consider:

- camera shots, positions and angles
- soundtrack
- the voice-over
- the portrayal of conflicts in which the animals are involved.

B Now use the table below to note down examples of how the audience may have been put in a position to identfy with the animals who are 'starring' in the show.

Method	How the audience is positioned
Camera shots, positions and angles	1. 2. 3.
Soundtrack	1. 2. 3.
Voice-over	1. 2. 3.
How conflicts with other animals/people are portrayed	1. 2. 3.

 C 1. Do you think the representation of the animals in the programme is fair and accurate?

2. Do you think it is easier to position the audience in sympathy with some animals than with others?

58-75

Conditions of consumption

A Using the table below, make a list of all examples of the media, or equipment for accessing the media, that are available for use at home. You obviously need to include any newspapers or magazines (just current issues) that are lying around, but also list such things as televisions (there may be more than one), radios (don't forget in the car), computers and hi-fi (including portable equipment).

In the second column, indicate roughly when each item is used. In the last column, decide who you think controls each item most of the time. For example, who decides what to watch on a television? (You may like to spend an evening seeing who is in charge of the remote control at any one time.)

Medium		Item and location	When used	By whom
Print	1.			
	2.			
	3.			
	4.			
	5.			
Television	1.			
	2.			
	3.			
	4.			
	5.			
Radio	1.			
	2.			
	3.			
	4.			
	5.			
Hi-fi	1.			
	2.			
	3.			
	4.			
	5.			
Computer	1.			
	2.			
	3.			
	4.			
	5.			

B Does control or ownership of the media in your home change during the course of a day? If so, try to explain why this is.

C Does access to different media change according to the time of day? For example, does the main television set in the house get watched by certain individuals at certain times of day?

D What effect do you think media consumption has on the relationships between the people in your home? Do you feel that the media is a force that brings people together, or one that separates them?

77-93

Your local cinemas

A How many cinemas are there in your local area? Find or draw a map of your local area, showing the cinemas that are within travelling distance.

B Choose two local cinemas and fill in the following chart.

	1.	2.
Name of cinema		
Street/town		
Type of cinema (e.g. arthouse, mainstream)		
Single screen, multiplex?		
Owner		
Types of film shown		
Number of screens		
Facilities (foyer, popcorn etc.)		
Specialist facilities (e.g. sound system, screen size)		

Media Studies for GCSE Teaching Pack

The top five films

Student's Book
77-93

A Which films are most popular in your area? Fill in the following chart for the top five films – those showing in most cinemas locally. (The top line has been filled in to show you how to do it.)

Name of film	Genre	Country of origin	Certificate	Type of audience
The Lord of the Rings	*Fantasy*	*NZ/US*	*PG*	*Family*
1.				
2.				
3.				
4.				
5.				

B Which of these films do you think will attract the largest audience? Give your reasons.

....

....

....

C Are minority interests catered for in your area? For example, are children's films or Asian films easily accessible?

....

....

....

....

....

Viewing conditions

A Going to the cinema is only one way of watching a film. Make a list of the ways in which seeing a film at the cinema is different from watching it on your television screen.

1. ....

....

2. ....

....

3. ....

....

4. ....

....

B Here are some ways in which you are likely to watch a film at home. After each example, write down how you think your viewing a film in that situation is likely to affect your enjoyment of it.

1. A film broadcast on BBC television

....

....

2. A film shown on commercial terrestrial channels (ITV, Channel 4 or Channel 5)

....

....

3. A film transmitted on a satellite channel

....

....

4. A video or DVD rented from the local video shop

....

....

5. A video or DVD that you have bought

....

....

6. A pay-per-view film on satellite TV

....

....

My ideas for a movie

A Choose a genre of film that you think is popular with audiences.

....

B Write down some of the features that you think audiences expect to see in a film of that genre.

1. ....

2. ....

3. ....

4. ....

5. ....

6. ....

C Now imagine you have the opportunity to make a film in the same genre.

1. Think of a title for your film.

....

2. Write in no more than 100 words a plot summary explaining what your film is about.

3. Using a storyboard sheet, design a short trailer for your film, to be shown at the cinema.

4. You might also like to design a poster to advertise your film.

5. Describe the sort of audience you think your film would appeal to. Why do you think they would enjoy it?

....

....

....

....

....

Marketing a film

A Choose a film that is about to be released at the cinema – the bigger the better. Write its name here.

....

B Keep a diary of the promotional activities that you notice in bringing the film to the attention of the audience. Collect cuttings related to the marketing of the film. For example, check on TV, radio, in newspapers and magazines for ways in which the film is promoted. Then answer these questions.

1. What different kinds of promotion were used?

....

....

....

....

....

2. What roles do the stars of the film play in promoting it?

....

....

....

3. Have you identified any spin-offs in the promotion of the film? How closely do you think these relate to the movie itself?

....

....

....

4. Is there any significance in the time of year that the film has been released?

....

....

5. Can you think of any ideas for promoting this film that you did not see being used?

....

....

....

94-109

Website publications

A Choose a website for any newspaper, magazine or comic that you have seen in print. Now compare the site with a current issue of the print version, by attempting the following tasks.

1. Explain what differences there are between the website and the print version.

....

....

....

....

....

2. Which do you think contains the more information?

....

3. List some of the advantages of being able to gain access through a website.

a) ....

b) ....

c) ....

4. Do you think the existence of a website will stop audiences buying print copies? Give your reasons.

....

....

....

....

B 1. Imagine that you run a website listings service for your local area. In addition to details of what's on, list some of the other items you would include in your site.

a) ....

b) ....

c) ....

d) ....

e) ....

2. Sketch a design for the home page of this website.

Using new technology

Consider each of the media activities listed below. For each, write down what sort of equipment you use. Then for each one write down what sort of equipment you would most like to use. Explain why you think this equipment would improve your enjoyment.

Listening to music

....

....

....

....

....

Watching films

....

....

....

....

Surfing the net

....

....

....

....

Using a mobile telephone

....

....

....

....

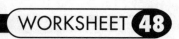

Technology on the move

The mobile phone is increasingly seen as an essential communication tool. It is becoming an important tool in the world of media. Mobile phones can use broadband technology so that users can watch a movie on their phone. Advertisers can send text messages to users telling them of the latest offers. News updates can be programmed to keep people up to date with the latest national and international events.

Imagine you have one of the latest mobile phones. Think about what sort of information you would want it to make available to you. Think also about the things you would prefer not to know about. Write your ideas in the boxes below:

Things I would want to hear about:

e.g. football scores
....
....
....
....
....
....
....
....

Things I wouldn't want to hear about:

e.g. Posh's latest single
....
....
....
....
....
....
....
....

Where will technology lead us?

Media technology is developing at an ever-increasing pace. Looking forward over the next ten years, try to imagine some of the ways that you think technology will change the way we consume the media. Under of each of the headings, write down your ideas for what changes will taker place.

At school: Teachers replaced by interactive monitors and headphones for each student. Detention issued by e-mail.

At home:

....

Watching television

....

Listening to music

....

Reading a magazine

....

Listening to the radio

....

One the move:

....

Using a computer

....

Using a mobile phone

....

Going to the cinema

....

Student's Book 110-139

Types of newspapers

A Use the grid below to identify some of the different types of newspaper that people read. Complete the first two sections with details of national newspapers, and the remainder with details of regional or local newspapers.

Title	Price	Circulation (copies sold per day)	Typical reader	Owner
National: broadsheet				
1.				
2.				
3.				
4.				
National: tabloid				
1.				
2.				
3.				
4.				
Regional: daily/evening				
1.				
2.				
Regional: weekly				
1.				
2.				
Regional: freesheet				
1.				

B 1. How many newspapers are brought into your home every week?

2. Make a list of all the titles, and next to each one, write down who reads them.

3. Which ones do you enjoy reading most?

Student's Book 116-139

FRONT PAGE

Look carefully at the front page of any of the newspapers you have identified in Worksheet 50, and consider how the layout of the page might encourage the reader to look at it in a certain way.

Make notes on your answers to the questions below as the basis for a class discussion.

A 1. How is the page is organised? Does the reader's eye move in particular direction, for example, from the masthead at the top of the page downwards?

B 1. How many different sizes and styles of lettering is there on the page? Make a list of these.

2. How do they signal to the reader the importance of each element of the page?

C 1. Where are the pictures placed on the page?

2. How important are they in grabbing your attention?

3. What sort of captions do they have?

4. How do they relate to the stories?

D 1. Do you think the front page is successful in attracting people to look at the newspaper?

2. Could it be improved? If so, how?

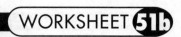

Look at the extracts taken from tabloid articles below. Work in groups to see if you can come up with your own headlines for these stories. Your teacher will then let you know what the originals were. Do you think that yours are better than the original?

1.

Police canteen chef Lisa Ryder has gone from being a pudding to a tasty dish. In just 18 months she has slimmed from 16st 2lb and 44D-40-46 to her present 10st 6lb and 36B-29-35.

Lisa, 32, from Rotherham, South Yorkshire, put on weight when she spent two years at catering college.

She recalls: "My family are all big and I'd always struggled with my weight".

Headline

2.

Deaf as a post Matt Hughes spent his wedding night in the nick after neighbours reported him for yelling at his bride.

They called the cops fearing that Matt and his missus were set to come to blows. But Matt ALWAYS speaks up because of his condition. Louise SHOUTS to make sure he has heard properly. And BOTH were louder than normal after "drinking heartily" at their reception.

Headline

3.

Girls will be judged on their brains as well as their beauty in this weeks first politically-correct Miss World contest.

Out go the blonde bimbos and ambitions to "work with children and animals". In come smart stunners with university degrees degree and good career prospects.

Among the 96 girls taking part in Friday's contest is an organic chemistry lecturer (Miss Antigua), a dentist (Miss Bolivia) and a psychologist (Miss Costa Rica).

Headline

Analysing a newspaper story

Choose a story from any of the newspapers you have looked at. It is probably best to choose the lead story from one of the pages. Now answer the following questions.

A In one sentence, say what the story is about.

....

....

....

B Do you think the story was one that the reporter knew was going to happen, or was it unexpected?

....

C Where do you think the information for the story came from?

....

D 1. Does the story use a picture? If so, how does this relate to the story being told?

....

....

2. Do you think it helps in our understanding of the story? If so, why?

....

....

E 1. How is the information in the story organised? For example, what information is given in the introduction or first paragraph?

....

....

....

....

....

....

2. Does the story have 'quotes' in it? ....

3. How many paragraphs is it divided into? ....

F 1. Do we know who wrote the story? Where can this information be found?

....

....

Who does what in newspapers?

On the left are some jobs that people do in newspapers. Match up these jobs with the job descriptions on the right. The first one has been done for you.

1 ■ news vendor

2 ■ editor

3 ■ reporter

4 ■ photographer

5 ■ advertising manager

6 ■ advertising telesales assistant

7 ■ news editor

8 ■ trainee reporter

9 ■ sub-editor

10 ■ pictures editor

11 ■ features editor

12 ■ designer

13 ■ distribution manager

14 ■ print manager

a ☐ *produces graphics for features and advertisements*

b ☐ *takes pictures*

c ☐ *decides what pictures are needed*

d ☐ *has responsibility for all advertising*

e ☐ *sells the newspaper on the street*

f ☐ *decides what stories should be covered*

g ☐ *obtains information and writes stories*

h ☐ *organises the layout of the paper, and checks the facts in the stories*

i ☐ *makes sure that the paper goes out to customers*

j ☐ *sells advertisements on the telephone*

k ☐ *is responsible for the overall content of the paper*

l ☐ *is learning to be a journalist*

m ☐ *controls the production of copies of the paper*

n ☐ *is responsible for articles that take a more in-depth look at issues*

Student's Book 110-139

Types of magazines

A Choose a type of magazine from the following list:

- women's
- sports
- television
- health
- teenage
- music
- film.

B Try to find four titles that you think fit into the genre you have chosen. Fill in the table below with the information that you discover about them. In the box at the end, explain what you think the appeal of each magazine is to the target audience.

Title	Circulation (no. sold)	Price	Target audience
1.			
Appeal:			
2.			
Appeal:			
3.			
Appeal:			
4.			
Appeal:			

C Imagine that you have been asked to produce a new title to compete in the existing market. Provide some details of your magazine under the following headings.

1. Title

....

2. Price

....

3. Target audience

....

D How would you make your magazine different in order to appeal to your readers?

....

....

....

....

....

         Media Studies for GCSE Teaching Pack

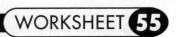

Cover and contents

Look carefully at the cover and contents page of a magazine.

A Cover

1. What information does the cover give you about what the magazine contains?

....

....

2. What do the following convey to the potential reader?

a) the title

....

b) the illustration on the cover

....

3. a) Do you think the cover will appeal to a potential reader?

....

b) How is it similar to titles in the same genre? How is it different?

....

....

....

B Contents page

1. Look carefully at the contents page. How far does it reinforce the information given on the cover of the magazine?

....

....

2. Make a short list of the types of article that are in the magazine. How do you think these will appeal to its readers?

a) ....

b) ....

c) ....

d) ....

e) ....

3. Imagine you are launching a new magazine to compete with the title you have just looked at. Design a cover and contents page for this new magazine. Make sure that they will appeal to the target audience.

Types of comics

A In the grid below, identify some of the comics that are currently published.

TITLE	GENRE	PRICE	PUBLISHER
FOR ADULTS			
1.			
2.			
3.			
4.			
5.			
6.			
FOR CHILDREN			
1.			
2.			
3.			
4.			
5.			
6.			

B Looking at some of the titles you have chosen, how do comics relate to other media products? For example, are some spin-offs of films or television programmes? Have any comics produced spin-offs in another media?

C Why do you think that comics still have a wide appeal when other forms of media might well have replaced them? What can they do that other media find more difficult?

Codes and conventions in comics

 A Look at the comic strip supplied by your teacher. Now answer briefly the following questions.

1. What are the narrative conventions that you can identify in the comic strip?

....

....

....

....

2. Describe the main characteristics of the images in the comic strip.

....

....

....

3. What do you notice about the characters? How does this relate to the conventions of portraying character in other comic strips that you have seen?

....

....

....

....

4. What devices are used to tell the reader how the words should be read? How do the words in the comic strip link to the images?

....

....

....

....

 B Try to devise your own comic strip. You may like to base it on an existing television programme or film.

- Explain briefly who the main characters might be.

- Give an example of a storyline involving those characters that might be used.

- If you are good at drawing, you might like to produce some sample frames for the comic.

The music in your life

A How much is music part of your life? Using the grid below, keep a log over the period of a single day of all the music that you hear. Use it to determine the type of music that you heard, the context in which you heard it, and whether it is music you chose to listen to or music that you had no choice but to hear.

Type of music	Context	Length of time	Did you choose to listen?
1.			
2.			
3.			
4.			
5.			
6.			
7.			
8.			
9.			
10.			

B What does the information you have gathered tell you about the part music plays in your life?

....

....

....

....

Popular music

Student's Book 140-159

A Choose a performer or band currently enjoying popularity. It doesn't matter whether you like their music yourself or not. Now try to find, and if possible collect, as much information as you can about them – for example, articles in newspapers and magazines, appearance and interviews on TV and radio, and information on websites.

The band/performer I have chosen is called:

....

B Now, based on the information you have collected, try to answer the following questions.

1. Why do you think the band/performer is popular?

....

....

2. Do you think their music is targeted at a specific group of people? If so, which group?

....

....

3. What image do you think they are trying to create through their music and the way they are represented in the media?

....

....

....

4. How, if at all, do you think they influence their fans in terms of the following:

● clothing ....

● attitude ....

● lifestyle? ....

5. Is there evidence to suggest that they encourage a certain type of media coverage in order to enhance their image? List some examples of this.

a) ....

b) ....

c) ....

d) ....

6. Why do you think people join fan clubs? Are you in one? Why?

....

....

....

My music

Student's Book 140-159

A Begin this worksheet by looking at your own CD/tape collection, or that of a member of your family. Organise this into different types of music, using the table below, by identifying what you think are the distinguishing features of the music, and describing briefly what sort of person listens to it.

Type of music	Distinguishing characteristics	Audience
1.		
2.		
3.		
4.		
5.		
6.		

B Now answer the following questions.

1. Does your collection contain music that you no longer listen to? Explain why you have stopped listening.

....

....

....

2. Do you listen to certain types of music at certain times? If so, describe briefly your listening pattern, and explain why you use music like this.

....

....

....

....

3. Are there any items in your collection that you feel ashamed to admit you own? If so, explain how you came to possess them.

....

....

4. What do you think a stranger would assume about your lifestyle if they were to look through your collection?

....

....

Promoting a new band

A Choose one of the types of music that you identified in Worksheet 60.

Type of music chosen:

....

B Imagine that you have been asked by a recording company to help with the launch of a new band whose music is of this type.

The company want to ensure that the band and their music have an appeal to a wider audience than simply the people who normally listen to this type of music. So they have asked you to come up with the following ideas.

1. Think of a name for the band.

....

2. What sort of image do you think the band should try to create in order to ensure they are popular with a cross-section of young people?

....

....

3. Identify three ways in which the band might promote a new single they are about to release.

a) ....

b) ....

c) ....

4. Using the storyboard sheet (Worksheet 9), sketch out some ideas for a promotional video that the band could release for broadcasting on music programmes on terrestrial and satellite TV.

5. Do you think the band are likely to be successful? Give reasons for your answer.

....

....

The music press

A Why do you think people read the music press?

B Choose three newspapers or magazines dedicated to popular music which are read by people of your age group, and fill in the table below.

Title of magazine	Type of consumer	Appeal to the reader
1.		
2.		
3.		

C Choose one of these titles and look at the section that deals with reviews of either new releases or live music.

1. What information is given in the reviews?

....

....

....

2. What use do you think this information is to the audience?

....

D Now write your own review, for inclusion in the magazine, of any concert you have been to recently, or any piece of recorded music you have heard. There is space in the magazine for only 100 words.

....

....

....

....

....

....

....

....

....

....

140-159

Compilation album

Imagine that you have been given the opportunity by a record company to put together a compilation album. The album, to be released on CD and tape, will consist of an hour of tracks based around a specific theme, for example 'The World's Saddest Love Songs'.

A To help you decide just what your album will sound like, have a go at completing the grid below. Remember, when you write out your list of tracks, that this is the order in which they will be heard. You need to strike a balance between different tracks, for example slow and upbeat, male and female vocals.

Theme of the album:

Title:

Track	Title	Timing
1		
2		
3		
4		
5		
6		
7		
8		
9		
10		
11		
12		
13		
14		
15		
16		
17		
18		
19		
20		

B Now design a cover for the CD version of the album. Don't forget to include your title and the list of tracks.

C Describe briefly the kind of audience that you think your album will appeal to.

Advertising record

160-173

A Use this worksheet to find out how many advertisements you are in contact with in a 24-hour period. Each time you see or hear an advertisement, make a record of it in the grid below.

When you have completed the grid, make a total for each and also make a grand total for the period as a whole.

Radio		Billboard	
Television		Internet	
Print		Other 1	
Cinema		Other 2	
Total		Total	
		GRAND TOTAL	

B Does the amount of advertising you have been in contact with surprise you? Give your reasons.

....

....

....

C 1. Now write down a list of advertisements that you remember seeing in each media.

2. Does any one advertisement stick in your mind? If so, describe it.

....

3. Where did you see it?

....

4. Why do you think it is memorable?

....

....

....

....

Targeting adverts

Student's Book 160-173

A 1. Think back to the information you collected in your survey in Worksheet 77. List any ads that you feel might have been targeted at you (that is, those ads promoting a product or service that you might want to buy). They may be some of those you identified in Task C.

a) ....

b) ....

c) ....

d) ....

e) ....

f) ....

2. Now list any you remember that were definitely not targeted at you.

a) ....

b) ....

c) ....

d) ....

e) ....

f) ....

3. Does the result suggest that advertisers are careful in targeting people to whom they wish to sell?

....

....

B If you were in charge of an advertising campaign, in which media and when do you think would be the best time to promote the following products? Fill in the table (the first one has been done for you).

Subject of campaign	Media	Timing
A soft drink	*TV*	*During Breakfast TV*
A luxury car		
A CD compilation of 60s chart hits		
Sheltered housing		
Holidays for 18–30 year olds		
A new type of baby food		

Advertising campaign

A Imagine that you have been asked to come up with ideas for one of the campaigns listed in Worksheet 65 (Task B). Have a go at the following tasks.

1. Devise a storyboard for a 30-second advertisement to be shown on television.

2. Produce a script for a radio advertisement of the same length.

3. Design an advertisement to be included in an appropriate magazine, or to be used as a billboard.

B Explain why you think your ideas would be appropriate for the target audience.

....

....

....

....

....

....

C Which media do you think is going to be the most effective in reaching your target audience? Explain why.

....

....

....

....

....

....

Student's Book 160-173

Hidden advertising

A Here are some types of 'covert' or hidden advertising. After each one, write down an example that you may have come across.

1. Product placement

....

....

2. Sponsorship

....

....

3. Advertorials

....

....

4. Endorsement

....

....

B Choose one of the examples you have found. Why do you think that the advertiser has chosen this method of promoting the goods or service?

....

....

....

....

....

C Choose one of these types of hidden advertising and say how you would use it to promote the product you worked on in Worksheet 79. Do you think it would be effective?

....

....

....

....

....

Controlling advertising

A Most advertising is subject to some form of control or regulation. Identify the organisation responsible for controlling advertisements in the following media.

1. Television:

....

2. Radio:

....

3. Billboards:

....

4. Newspapers:

....

5. Magazines:

....

B Imagine that the following advertisement has appeared in your local newspaper.

RUMPOLE'S YUMMY GUM

Tests have shown that people under the age of sixteen who don't chew Rumpole's Yummy Gum:

✻ Don't have any friends   ✻ Never get invited to parties

✻ Are considered unattractive   ✻ Fail all of their exams

So if you wants lots of friends, who think you are attractive and invite you to their parties, get Rumpole's Yummy Gum – it will even make sure you pass your Media Studies exam.

Write a letter of complaint to the appropriate body, outlining what you think is wrong with the advertisement, and suggesting what should be done about it.

Listening to the radio

Student's Book 174-191

A Make a list of all the radio stations that you know you can receive in the area where you live.

B Use a radio to tune to all of the frequencies on which stations are broadcasting between 88 and 108 MHz. Each time you find a station, mark its location, with its name.

C Now listen to it long enough to fill in details of each station you have found on the chart below.

Station	Commercial/ BBC	Local/ national	Type of music/talk	Audience
1.				
2.				
3.				
4.				
5.				
6.				
7.				
8				
9.				
10.				

D Now compare your first list (Task A) with your second (Task C).

1. Are there any stations that you did not know you could receive?

....

2. Are there any stations you thought you could receive, but you found you could not? Why do you think this is so?

....

3. Which stations do you think you would most like to listen to some more?

....

4. Which stations would you definitely not want to listen to again?

....

....

Radio station profile

Choose a radio station that you find interesting. It can either be one you normally listen to, or one you know little about. However, you will need to listen to the station at different times of day and night in order to find out as much as you can about it. Now complete the details below about the station.

1. Name of station

....

2. Style of presentation

....

....

3. Type of output

....

....

....

4. Speech/music: details of type

....

....

....

5. Schedules: does it appeal to the same audience throughout the day?

....

....

....

6. Identity: how is the identity of the station established?

....

....

7. What sort of audience do you think the station aims to attract?

....

....

8. Why do you think that this station does or does not appeal to its audience?

....

....

....

91

174-191

A new station 1: Identity

Imagine that you have been asked to help with developing a new local radio station that will have a broad audience appeal to people in your local area. You should bear in mind that it is designed to attract listeners with a variety of interests from all ages and backgrounds, and that it will have to compete with existing local BBC and commercial stations.

Fill in the sheet below with your ideas for the station under the following headings:

1. Choose a name for your station that will establish a sense of local identity.

2. Design a logo for the station.

3. Explain briefly what sort of programmes the station should broadcast.

4. Explain the other ways in which you would give the station an identity. You may like suggest ideas for jingles and slogans, for example.

Station name

Logo

Types of programme/schedules | Identity

1

2

3

4

174-191

A new station 2: Pilot broadcast

Your new station has been given permission to run a series of pilot broadcasts next month. You have been asked to put together a one-hour programme on a Friday evening that will appeal to an audience of 15 to 25 year olds. The programme must be divided equally between music and talk.

A Describe briefly the style of the programme you would want to broadcast. Suggest some ideas for the content of the programme, including the types of music you might play, as well as details of any studio guests or similar items.

....

....

....

....

....

....

B Now use the grid below to give details of exactly how you would fill this one-hour slot. In the first column, give the timings; in the second column, give details of what each section would contain. The first entry has been given as an example.

Timings	Contents
00:00 to 01:30	Introduction, details of guests etc.

Student's Book 174-191

A new station 3: Promotion

Before the radio station is launched, it needs to be promoted to the local community.

A Using any of the material you have created in Worksheets 71 and 72, devise a storyboard for an advertisement to be shown on regional commercial television promoting the new station. (You may like to use the template in Worksheet 9.)

B Design a display advertisement for inclusion in a local newspaper, giving information about the new station.

C Write down three other ideas suggesting how the station might be promoted.

1. ....

....

2. ....

....

3. ....

....

D Of all these ideas, which do you think is likely to be the most successful, and why?

....

....

....

....

....

Types of TV news

192-203

Look at the news bulletin that your teacher shows you, and attempt the following tasks.

 A Using the categories in the first column of the table below, think carefully about each story and decide which category it fits best. For each category choose a story from the bulletin as an example, writing a brief description in the second column. Then, in the third column, explain why you think it fits the category.

■ Category of news	■ Example story	■ Why story fits category
1. Hard news		
2. Political news		
3. International news		
4. Human interest news		
5. Celebrity news		
6. Sports news		

 B 1. Do some stories fit into more than one category?

    2. Are there stories that don't fit into any category? If so, make up a category that you think is appropriate.

  C 1. Which of the stories that appear in the bulletin do you think were not expected by the news team? How can you tell?

    2. Which do you think the news team knew about in advance and were able to prepare for? How can you tell?

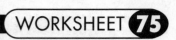

News coverage on TV

A Using a listings magazine or a newspaper, calculate how many hours of news there are in 24 hours of TV on all the main channels. Your teacher will allocate your group a particular day to investigate. Put the results in the second column in the chart below.

B Then fill in the third column of the table to show the proportion of the day that is devoted to news. You will probably need a calculator to help you work out the percentages.

Channel	Number of hours of news on _____ day	Percentage of day filled with news
☐ BBC 1		
☐ BBC 2		
☐ ITV		
☐ Channel 4		
☐ Channel 5		
☐ Sky News		
☐ Cable		

C Compare your findings and work out what is the average news coverage on each channel on each day.

Student's Book
192-203

A close look at a news story

Take a close look at any of the stories you have worked on as part of this unit, and have a go at the following tasks.

A Explain in one sentence what the story is about.

....

....

....

B 1. What position does the story occupy in the running order of the bulletin?

....

2. Why do you think it was placed there?

....

....

3. How long does the story run for?

....

C Describe how the story is told.

1. Who tells the story – the news presenter in the studio, a reporter at the scene, or a voice-over?

....

2. What visual images are used to tell the story? Don't forget to mention graphics or still images.

....

....

....

3. How important do you think these visuals are to the telling of the story?

....

....

4. Is the story told from a particular viewpoint? For example, does it give a balanced view of two sides, or does it seem to favour one viewpoint?

....

....

....

....

Student's Book 192-203

TV news running order

A Look at the news stories below, and the information about the visual material that is available to go with each story. It is your job to decide on the order in which these stories would be broadcast in a five-minute bulletin on the evening news around 6.00 p.m.. You should bear in mind that there will be a family audience for this news, consisting of both adults and young people.

a.
Story: Forty-vehicle motorway pile-up in Leicestershire, including party of school-children travelling in a minibus. Three people known to have died. Thirty may be injured.

Visual material: Aerial view of accident. Interview with rescue worker. Shots of ambulances arriving at local hospital. Eye-witness interview.

b.
Story:
Lead singer of Venus, a chart-topping all-girl band, missing in Australia during tour of the country. Walked out after argument with another band member. Car she was driving in found abandoned in remote spot.
Visual material:
Footage of previous night's gig. Interview with boyfriend. Tearful fans. Interview with other band members. Police spokesman expresses concern for safety.

c.
■ **Story:** Britain's largest building society has increased its lending rate. Mortgages to cost more.

■ **Visual material:** Graphic showing cost of average mortgage. Interview with building society chief. Vox pop of reactions in a London street.

d.
Story Prince Charles opens a new hospital in Africa, built with donations from British charities.

Visual material Video of opening ceremony.

e.
STORY
British heart-throb teenage actor detained at customs in New York, allegedly in possession of illegal drugs.

VISUAL MATERIAL
Clip of star receiving award for role in latest film.

B After you have decided where each story would go, give your reasons for putting it in that position in the running order.

1ST story = ☐ because ....

2ND story = ☐ because ....

3RD story = ☐ because ....

4TH story = ☐ because ....

5TH story = ☐ because ....

Writing a news script

Student's Book 192-203

Write the script for the news story below as part of a TV news bulletin aimed at teenagers, broadcast at 5.00 p.m. on a weekday. Remember that the script should include not only the words that explain to the viewer what the story is about, but also the camera shots that you will need for your report.

> Lead singer of Venus, a chart-topping all-girl band, missing in Australia during tour of the country. Walked out after argument with another band member. Car she was driving in found abandoned in remote spot.

Use the additional information below. Add any detail that you feel is appropriate.

> Other band members plead with her to get in touch. They are very upset after argument.

> Singer's name is Zelda G. Car found abandoned, out of petrol, 50 miles from gig venue.

> Venus are top of the charts in the UK. They are about to star in their own film, due for release next month.

> Tearful Venus fans want Zelda to come back so band can finish sell-out tour.

> Zelda walked out on a previous occasion last year but returned unharmed a week later, refusing to say where she had been.

> Police are worried that a young woman should be on her own in a remote and potentially dangerous part of the country.

> Tour manager apologises to fans. Tour will have to be postponed. People who bought tickets to get a refund.

> Boyfriend Barry, motorcycle racing champion, interviewed in California. He's desperately worried and is flying straight out to help look for her.

WORKSHEET **79**

204-229

Production planning sheet 1

Complete the table below to help you consider your approach to your production.

Title of your proposed production

....

A Resources **1.** What equipment will you need for your production?

....

....

2. List other resources you will need, such as locations (e.g. someone's lounge).

....

....

....

B Skills **1.** What relevant skills do you already possess?

....

2. List the skills that you need to learn.

....

....

C Medium **1.** What medium are you going to work in?

....

2. Explain why this is the best medium.

....

....

D Audience What is the audience for your product? Be as precise as possible.

....

E Group work **1.** Are you intending to work as a group?

....

2. If so, list the individual members and their responsibilities.

....

....

....

F Research List examples of similar media products that you intend to look at, to help
guide your own production.

....

....

....

Production planning sheet 2

Use this sheet to outline how your production will relate to the key concepts you have studied in other parts of your course.

A Language

How will the language of your production reflect or contrast with the language used in similar media products? Remember that 'language' in this context refers to far more than the words you may use.

....

....

....

....

....

B Representation

What will be represented in your production, and from whose viewpoint?

....

....

....

....

....

C Institutions

1. What is the market in which the product will be consumed?

....

2. Is it already established, e.g. an existing TV slot or magazine? Or have you invented one of your own, e.g. a new breakfast radio show?

....

3. Are there any restrictions on what you are allowed to include?

....

D Audience

1. What is the primary audience?

....

2. How is it made up?

....

3. Is there a secondary audience?

....

4. How will they be addressed?

....

---

101 Media Studies for GCSE Teaching Pack

WORKSHEET 81a

204-229

Production planning sheet 3: video production

This worksheet is designed to help you organise the jobs you need to do in order to complete a video production. Where you are working as a group, it will provide a reminder to individual group members of the specific responsibilities that they have been allocated.

Date	Task	Resources needed	Whose responsibility	Completed Y/N
	1. Research (finding information, locations)			
	2. Scripting			
	3. Shooting/recording			
	4. Logging shots			
	5. Editing script			
	6. Soundtrack			
	7. Titles/graphics			
	8. Editing			
	9. Packaging			

Production planning sheet 3: sound/radio production

This worksheet is designed to help you organise the jobs you need to do in order to complete a sound/radio production. Where you are working as a group, it will provide a reminder to individual group members of the specific responsibilities that they have been allocated.

Date	Task	Resources needed	Whose responsibility	Completed Y/N
	1. Research (arranging interviews, studio guests)			
	2. Scripting			
	3. Finding materials (music, archive material)			
	4. Recording			
	5. Editing/mixing			
	6. Packaging			

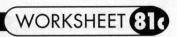

Production planning sheet 3: print production

This worksheet is designed to help you organise the jobs you need to do in order to complete a print production. Where you are working as a group, it will provide a reminder to individual group members of the specific responsibilities that they have been allocated.

Date	Task	Resources needed	Whose responsibility	Completed Y/N
	1. Research			
	2. Planning (arranging interview, photographs)			
	3. Drafting			
	4. Writing/keyboarding			
	5. Photos/illustrations			
	6. Design work			
	7. Page layout			
	8. Printing/collating			

Production sheet

PRODUCTION SHEET

Visual instructions (type of shot/camera movement)	Sound instructions (music/sound effects)	Dialogue	Setting/location/action	Timing

Shot list

Shot no.	Brief description of shot required	Location	Date/time	Special information	Completed
	Mandy getting out of parked car	*High Street*	*19 April 2.30 pm*	*Must be wearing green anorak*	✔
1.					
2.					
3.					
4.					
5.					
6.					
7.					
8.					
9.					
10.					

   Media Studies for GCSE Teaching Pack

Log sheet for video

By using this log sheet, you can save a lot of time searching through your tapes for scenes that you need for the final edit. You will have to use a video player or edit suite with a 'real-time' counter in minutes and seconds. Make sure that your tape is fully rewound, and that the counter is set to zero, before you start.

Description of shot	Timing	Usable?	Action
Tessa walking the dog	01:33 to 04:56	✓	nil
Paul looking out of window	06:41 to 07:33	✗	re-shoot
1.			
2.			
3.			
4.			
5.			
6.			
7.			
8.			
9.			
10.			

Editing sheet

Before you start editing your video production, you need to have a clear idea of what sequences to use and the order you want to put them in. Use this sheet, together with your log sheets, to prepare your edit script.

Shot/sequence	Sound	Position on tape	Length of shot	Edit
Sun rising over mountains	Grieg's 'Morning'	03:22	5 secs	dissolve
Dave on motorbike		21:29	10 secs	cut
1.				
2.				
3.				
4.				
5.				
6.				
7.				
8.				
9.				
10.				

WORKSHEET 86

Design sheet for magazine/newspaper

204-229

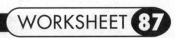 WORKSHEET **87**

204-229

Production diary

Filling in this diary will provide you with a useful record of the work you have planned and undertaken. Remember to complete your diary at the end of each session of work on the practical production. The record of your decisions will provide useful material when you come to write your supporting account – this is especially important with group production work, to prevent later misunderstanding.

Session no:	Date:
Work planned for session	
Equipment used	
What was achieved	
If this differed from what was planned, why?	
Summary of key decisions made	
Activities planned in preparation for next session	
Comments	

Thinking about the supporting account

Student's Book 204-229

You can use this worksheet to help you gather together the material and ideas that you are going to need for writing your supporting account.

A Context

1. What context have you decided is the most appropriate for your production, e.g. which television channel, at what time?

2. Why have you chosen this context?

3. Looking at what you have produced, do you think that your production will be right for this slot?

B Audience

1. Do you think the audience you have identified for your production will respond positively to it? If so, what do you think will appeal to them?

2. Do you think it might have a wider appeal than the audience you first identified?

C Purpose

1. What did you see as the main purpose of your production?

2. Do you think that it fulfils that purpose? Do you think your audience will agree?

D Evaluation

1. How successful do you think your production has been at meeting the intention you started out with?

2. Have you had any useful criticism from other people about the production?

3. Do you think the criticism is fair?

4. If you could undertake the production again, how would you change it to make it better (if at all)?

E Self-assessment

1. Do you feel you worked effectively on the production? You should consider such things as planning, organisation and time management.

2. What skills have you acquired or developed?

3. Did you enjoy working best on your own, or with others?

Presentation checklist

As your work may be marked by both your teacher and an examiner from the exam board, it is important that you organise and present it in such a way that it is easy to follow. Here is a checklist to help you make sure that you have done this.

1. Is the production in a logical and correct order (for example, magazine pages in sequence, all tapes cued up at the right place, work clearly labelled)? ☐

2. Is your name, date, centre number and candidate number clearly written on all the work? ☐

3. Is the planning and research work clearly organised and labelled? ☐

4. Are there enough illustrations? ☐

5. Are the diagrams and illustrations clearly captioned? ☐

6. Is the supporting account clearly identified and set out under appropriate headings? ☐

7. Have you covered all the key points in your supporting account? ☐

8. Are any diagrams, illustrations, appendices and bibliography in the supporting account properly organised and signposted? ☐

9. Have you kept within the recommended word limit for the supporting account (700–800 words)? ☐

10. Have you outlined details of group members and their responsibilities? ☐

204-229

Assignment brief

Media:	TV and magazine
Topic:	Television advertising

Key concepts: Media language, Representation	Assessment objectives: 1, 2 and 3 (weighting 1:2:2)

Using an advertisement that you have seen recently on the television as a starting point, undertake the following tasks:

1. Give a brief account of the style and content of the advertisement. Remember to consider such things as:

    ■ camera work
    ■ visual imagery
    ■ editing
    ■ sound (including dialogue, music, sound effects and voice-over)
    ■ narrative.

2. Explain how the roles that people play in the advertisement are represented, for example, the relationships between couples and within families. Do you think the representation is 'true to life'?

3. **a)** Using ten frames of a storyboard sheet, produce your own advertisement for the product, but reversing the roles represented in the original.

    b) Design a similar advertisement for the product to be included in an appropriate magazine. Give the name of the magazine in which it is to appear.

4. Explain why you think your advertisement would or would not be appropriate to promote the product on television and in the magazine.

Researching around the topic

Student's Book 230-239

The topic for the controlled test changes every year, but your teacher will be able to tell you what it is well in advance.

As soon as you know the topic, here is a checklist of things that you can do to help you prepare well in advance.

A Start a **research file** of materials relating to the topic. You can use:

- newspapers and magazines
- television programmes
- radio programmes
- the internet.

You could add video/audio tapes and computer disks to this file, where you think they would be useful.

B Spend some time **looking at a variety of examples** of the genre or form that has been specified. For example, if the topic is about popular music, try to get a wide view of different types of popular music and the audiences they appeal to. Try to avoid just using the test as an excuse to listen to music you are interested in, for example.

C **Think around the topic** a little. Consider how examples of the product are marketed, for instance, and what industries relate to it through spin-off products. You might, for example, look at the relationship between the output of radio stations and the music industry.

D Consider **working with another person or group** of people to arrange to share or swap the information and resources that you have collected. You may like to consider planning a class activity based on the topic area, using some of these materials.

WORKSHEET 92

The key concepts

In the controlled test you will need to show your knowledge of the key concepts that you have explored earlier in the course and in earlier worksheets. It is a good idea to have these in mind when you are doing any work on the topic area.

You can use the sheet below to jot down your ideas about how you think these concepts might apply to the topic you are studying.

YOUR TOPIC

Language

Representation

Institutions

Audience

Storyboard practice

A Your teacher will show you a short sequence from a television programme. While you are watching it, make a note of the following:

1. Different types of shot and camera angles used.

2. How the different shots or sequences are edited together.

3. Any dialogue or voice-over used.

4. Any music or sound effects used.

5. Any special effects used.

6. The length of time each shot or sequence lasts.

B Now draw the sequence, using the storyboard sheet (Worksheet 9), giving details of shots, edits, timings and sound (including music). It doesn't matter how good you are at drawing as long as you can make the images recognisable. Remember, however, to use colour where appropriate.

C Now imagine that you have been asked to come up with some ideas for a programme in a similar genre. Using another blank copy of Worksheet 9, produce your own 30-second storyboard for a trail for your programme. Give full details about the visuals, sound and timing, as you did in the first storyboard.

Using a production sheet (TV)

Student's Book 230-239

A Look at the notes you made in Worksheet 93 about the sequence you watched. (You may need to watch the sequence again.) This time try to produce a script for the sequence using the production sheet (Worksheet 82). You will have to think about how a shot or scene can be described in words instead of pictures.

B Using another production sheet, script the same 30-second trail that you produced in Worksheet 93.

C Now compare your efforts by filling in the sheet below. Give your reasons wherever possible.

1. How does your production sheet differ from the script on the storyboard?

....

....

....

....

....

2. Which did you find easier and quicker to do?

....

....

3. Which do you think conveys your ideas better?

....

....

4. Which do you think looks more effective?

....

....

5. Which method do you think will be easier for you to use in the controlled test if you are asked to produce a script?

....

....

Using a production sheet (radio)

Student's Book 230-239

A Listen to the extract from a radio broadcast that your teacher has recorded for you. Make some notes below on what you hear. Some headings have been given, so you can organise your notes.

1. Voice-over

....

....

2. Dialogue

....

....

3. Sound effects

....

....

4. Music

....

....

5. Length of time each sequence lasts

....

....

6. Editing – how the sequences are joined together

....

....

B Now use the production sheet (Worksheet 82) to script what you have heard, ignoring the column for visual instructions.

Designing a poster or advertisement

One skill you may need to use in the controlled test is designing a poster or advertisement. Use this worksheet to practise that skill.

 A Begin by looking at a selection of advertisements in a magazine, or some posters, for example advertisements for films. Choose one of these that interests you and make notes on the following:

1. What information is given?

....

....

2. What images are present? Are there people in the poster, for example? Are any colours or images particularly prominent?

....

....

....

3. What words are written? Are any devices used to make certain words stand out, e.g. larger lettering (point size) or bold letters?

....

....

....

4. How do the words and the images relate to one another?

....

....

....

5. In what context are you most likely to see the ad or poster?

....

....

B Now it is your turn to design a poster for a similar product.

- First make a checklist of what information you need to include.
- Think about what you have found from analysing the layout above before you design your own.
- Remember that your drawing skill is not important. It is the ideas and organisation of the material that matters most.

 C Now, by applying some of the questions above, evaluate how effective you have been in your own design.

Preparing to tackle the questions

Student's Book 230-239

Once you have been issued with the controlled test paper you should have time to do some research to prepare you for tackling the questions.

A Use the grid below to make a list of what you think you need to do (first column), when you intend to do it (second column) and where you need to go for the information (third column). The first item has been filled in as an example only!

Task	Time	Place
Find out which magazines are targeted at fans of dance music	*Tuesday 10:00 a.m.*	*Evans Newsagents, Charles St*

B Now make another list of products that you may find useful to give as examples when you respond to the questions. For example, a list of action films that you may want to refer to.

a) ....

b) ....

c) ....

d) ....

e) ....

Preparation checklist

When you have spent some time looking at the paper and thinking about the tasks that you have been asked to tackle, there are a number of things you can do to make sure you are fully prepared. When you have completed each of the jobs listed in the table below, tick the box or make a note of any further action you need to take.

	Completed?	Further action required
1. Make sure you understand what is required in each task	☐	
2. Decide which page of the answer book is best for answering each task and make a note of it	☐	
3. Check that you know how much time you have for each task (see Worksheet 99)	☐	
4. Make sure you know the time and date of each session, and how long it lasts	☐	
5. Get together all the necessary equipment (see Worksheet 101)	☐	
6. Have you researched the answers?	☐	
7. Have you planned the answers?	☐	
8. Have you practised the storyboards etc.?	☐	

WORKSHEET **99**

Timing the test

Student's Book 230-239

Using your copy of the question paper, it is a good idea to work out how much time you should spend on each task. Remember that you have a total of four hours in which to complete the test.

A Look at the number of marks given to each task. There is a total of 100 marks for the four tasks. In the table below, first of all write the number of marks awarded for each task in the second column.

(Of course, the paper may not always be organised in this way, so you may find that you don't have to fill in all of the spaces.)

Task	Marks awarded	Time to be allowed
1a		
1b		
1c		
1d		
2a		
2b		
2c		
2d		
3a		
3b		
3c		
3d		
4a		
4b		
4c		
4d		
TOTAL	100 marks	180 minutes

B You can work out the amount of time you should spend on each task by multiplying each mark available by 1.8 minutes. For example, a task worth 10 marks should be allowed 18 minutes (10 X 1.8 = 18). Now use the third column to indicate what time you should spend on each of the tasks.

C You may now like to plan how you are going to divide up this time within the different sessions when you will be taking the test. (See also Worksheet 101.)

Remember: you are advised to perform each task in the order given on the question paper.

Practising your presentation skills

A The controlled test is not like a traditional exam paper where you are asked to write essay responses.

Most likely you will be asked to work 'in role', which means pretending to play the part of someone who works in the media. In such a job, presentational skills are important, especially in getting ideas across clearly and accurately. So think about how best to present any information you are asked for.

B Now consider each of the tasks you are being asked to perform, and note down if any of the following devices may be able to help you.

	Task 1	Task 2	Task 3	Task 4
Headings				
Paragraphs				
Use of bullet points (●)				
Numbering (1.)				
Illustrations				
Underlining and italics				
UPPER and lower case lettering				
Colour coding				
Any other				

C Imagine that you are asked to give details of the key features of a particular genre, such as soap operas. Using any of the devices above that you feel would be appropriate, plan how you would organise your response to the question.

Test schedule and checklists

A Make sure you know exactly when and where each session of your test is going to be, by completing the form below. (The first line has been given as an example only!)

Session	Date	Time	Duration	Location
1	10 May	9.30	1 hour	Class 4R
1.				
2.				
3.				
4.				
5.				
6.				

B Before you go into each session, make sure you have the equipment you need. Here is a list of key items. Tick the box when you have got each one ready to take into the session.

☐ Pens   ☐ Eraser

☐ Pencils   ☐ Colouring pencils or felt tips

☐ Ruler   ☐ A head full of good ideas

C You should use the list below as a checklist for your last session of the controlled test. You cannot take it in with you, so you will need to memorise it.

Save ten minutes or so at the end of the test to check that you have done the following:

● **1.** Completed all the tasks fully

● **2.** Numbered the tasks correctly

● **3.** Made it clear where you have answered each part of a task (e.g. on storyboard or production sheets)

● **4.** Carefully attached and numbered any additional sheets you have used

● **5.** Made sure that it all makes sense

● **6.** Checked carefully that your spelling, punctuation and grammar are as good as you can make them.

Good luck!

Contacts and resources

AQA materials

In the first instance, probably the most useful materials teachers should consult are those produced by AQA itself. This is downloadable as a PDF file from the AQA website (www.aqa.org.uk)

Besides defining content and assessment requirements, the specification offers a definition of each of the key concepts, indicating clearly the depth to which these need to be explored. In addition, a matrix which links the assessment objectives, the key concepts and each of the major media forms provides detailed information about activities that can be used to steer students through the syllabus.

Banded performance criteria are provided in the specification to guide teachers in the assessment of coursework folders.

A support book is also available. This offers guidance in implementing a course, explains the administrative procedures and suggests strategies for assessing coursework folders. In addition, teachers may find useful the advice concerning the controlled test and tiering.

Specimen controlled test papers are available from the board, as are past 'live' papers.

Teachers in need of any of these materials should get in touch with the Subject Officer for Media Studies at AQA (01483 506506).

Suggested reading

For teachers new to Media Studies, and in need of a rapid introduction, the following books are particularly recommended:

O'Sullivan, Dutton, and Rayner, *Studying the Media: An Introduction* (Edward Arnold, 1994, 1998)
Rayner, Wall and Kruger, *Media Studies: The Essential Introduction* (Routledge, 2001)

Both provide a useful and comprehensive overview of the discipline.

In addition, teachers may find it helpful to consult a number of books that provide useful background and suggestions for teaching strategies. Most of these have been published over the past fifteen years and may seem a little dated now, but they all offer valuable advice.

L. Masterman, *Teaching the Media* (Routledge, 1985)
D. Lusted (ed.), *The Media Studies Book: A Guide for Teachers* (Routledge, 1987, 1991)
M. Alvarado, R. Gutch and T. Wollen, *Learning the Media* (Macmillan, 1987)

Teaching production is a problem area for many teachers. Obviously the most effective learning strategy for teachers themselves is hands-on experience. Sadly the reality is that this is not always possible given ever-increasing workloads. Teachers have to accept that a lot of their learning will have to take place alongside that of their students, who, in many cases, may climb the learning curve rather faster than teachers themselves.

There are a number of production books which offer guidance and support for production work. These include:

R. Stafford, *Hands On: A Teacher's Guide to Media Technology* (BFI, 1993)
R. Dimbleby, N. Dimbleby and K. Whittington, *Practical Media* (Hodder, 1994)

Organisations

A number of organisations exist which offer support to media teachers.

The Education Department of the **British Film Institute**, 21 Stephen Street, London W1T 1LN (0207 255 1444; www.bfi.org.uk/) can provide a catalogue of resources, including teaching packs. The BFI also organises conferences and other events.

Film Education, Alhambra House, 27–31 Charing Cross Road, London WC2H 0AU (0207 976 2291); www.filmeducation.org/) publishes and distributes teaching materials, including study guides for some films on general release. It is well worth getting on their mailing list.

English and Media Centre 18 Compton Terrace, London N1 2UN (0207 359 8080; www.englishandmedia.co.uk) A useful site dedicated to supporting teachers.

The **Northern Ireland Media Education Association**, Belvoir Primary School, Belvoir Drive, Belfast BT8 4DL (02890 491801) provides support for teachers in Northern Ireland.

A visit to the **National Museum of Photography, Film and Television**, Pictureville, Bradford BD1 1NQ (01274 727488) or the **Museum of the Moving Image**, South Bank, London SE1 8XT (0207 815 1337) can provide the basis for stimulating work for students at all levels.

Many large cities also have media centres offering a range of support activities for teachers and students.

INSET providers in the field of Media Studies include **Cornwall College**, Trinity Court, Southernhay East, Exeter EX1 1QG (01392 433599) and **Masterclasses**, Unit 9, The Tradebase, Catfield, Norfolk NR29 5AA (01692 582565; www.a-grades.com).

A number of the regulatory bodies can be sources of teaching and reference materials. Many of these use websites to update materials. They include:

Independent Television Commission, 33 Foley Street, London W1P 7TL (0207 255 3000; www.itc.org.uk/)
Broadcasting Standards Commission, 7 The Sanctuary, London SW1P 3JS (0207 808 1000; www.bsc.org.uk/)
Press Complaints Commission, 1 Salisbury Square, London EC4Y 8AE (0207 353 1248; www.pcc.org.uk)
Advertising Standards Authority, 2 Torrington Place, London WC1E 7HW (0207 580 5555; www.asa.org.uk/index.htm)
British Board of Film Classification, 3 Soho Square, London W1V 6HD (0207 440 1570; www.bbfc.co.uk/)
Radio Authority, Holbrook House, 14 Great Queen Street, London WC2B 5DG (0207 430 2724; www.radioauthority.org.uk/)

The function of several of these regulatory bodies are combined under the aegis of Ofcom (Office of Communications) from 2003. Website address: www.ofcom.gov.uk/

Other organisations that may be able to provide support and stimulus, especially through websites, are:

Campaign for Press and Broadcasting Freedom, CPBF, 2nd Floor, Vi and Garner Smith House, 23 Orford Road, Walthamstow, London E17 9NL (0208 521 5932); www.cpbf.org.uk

Internet

The Internet has become an effective means of keeping in touch with media education across the curriculum. A lot of material is probably pitched a little high for GCSE, but teachers themselves may well find that many of the sites listed are a valuable source of support, ideas and stimulation.

The best sites are those that also offer links to other sources of materials and ideas. Teachers using the Internet as a potential media education resource may find the following sites worth a visit:

The Internet Movies Database (www.imdb.com/). Excellent searchable site for information on cinema and the film industry.

The Media Unions' home page (gn.apc.org/media/) links to NUJ, BECTU etc.

Media UK (www.mediauk.com/directory/) offers useful links to TV, radio, newspaper and magazine industries.

Media Village (www.mediavillage.co.uk/) offers useful links to information about the media industries.

BARB (www.barb.co.uk/) provides access to TV audience figures.

Nearly all media organisations, such as national newspapers, television stations and magazines, have their own sites, all of variable value and quality. Probably the most effective way to access these is by typing in the name of the organisation into a search engine.

Sites well worth bookmarking include:

BBC (www.bbc.co.uk/)
The Guardian/Observer (www.guardian.co.uk/)
Press Association (www.pa.press.net/)
Channel 4 (www.channel4.co.com/)
The Times (www.thetimes.co.uk/)
Reuters (www.reuters.com/)
Mirror Group (www.mirrorgroup.co.uk/)
Sky (www.sky.com/)
ITV (www.itv.co.uk/)
Channel 5 (www.channel5.com/)

Other sites that teachers may find it useful to explore include:

ABC Home Page (www.abc.org.uk/) the Audit Bureau of Circulation, providing access to print circulation data.
CCMS (Communication, cultural and media studies) (www.cultsock.ndirect.co.uk/MUHome/cshtml) a user-friendly site packed with useful information.
MCS (Media and Communication Studies) (www.aber.ac.uk/media/Functions/mcs.html) comprehensive and detailed information on media theory.
National Readership Survey (www.nrs.co.uk/contents.cfm) provides extensive research into newspaper and magazine readership.
Newspapers in Education (www.nie.northcliffe.co.uk/) is a potential source of ideas and links.
Sarah Zupko's Cultural Studies Center (www.popcultures.com/) is high powered, but provides access to the ideas of leading cultural studies theorists.
Theory.Org.UK (www.theory.org.uk) cutting edge 'social theory for fans of populay culture'.